Tap Dancing

Rhythm in their Feet

RHYTHM OF A FOOT PERCUSSION ARTIST

I've got rhythm in my body, I've got rhythm in my feet
You can play around with rhythm if you stay within the beat
Take a crotchet or a quaver
Or some dotted notes, for flavour,
Mix the values, add an accent, and to make the phrase complete
Add a touch of syncopation
To the rhythmic combination
Keep it swinging through the measure, or to make it sound élite
Add a subtle change of tone
Soft or loud but not a drone
Then a phrase or two of stop-time or perhaps a plain repeat.

Fill the bar with sounds that ripple
Make it quadruple or triple
Use the rhythms felt innately and transfer them to the feet
Let the sounds be an incentive
To be more and more inventive
Keep the discipline of time because on this you cannot cheat.

There must also be some places
Where the rhythm has some spaces
Take a beat or two of silence in between each rattling feat.
Such advice is better heeded
For the silences are needed
To appreciate the contrast of a rippling, rhythmic treat.
It's a subject full of pleasure
Making rhythms you will treasure
So with rhythm in your body and with rhythm in your feet
You can share or trade creative sounds with all the friends you meet.

Tap Dancing

Rhythm in their Feet

Heather Rees

The Crowood Press

First published in 2003 by
The Crowood Press Ltd
Ramsbury, Marlborough
Wiltshire SN8 2HR

www.crowood.com

This impression 2005

© Heather Rees 2003

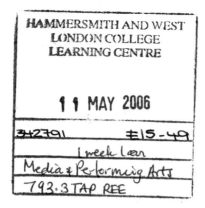
British Library Cataloguing-in-Publication Data
A catalogue record for this book is available from the British Library.

ISBN 1 86126 579 4

Dedication
To Arthur, to Mother and to Joy, with my love and thanks.

Acknowledgements
My grateful thanks to everyone who has helped, supported and encouraged me. For helping to find resource material: Mollie Web, ISTD Library, Bexhill Library, British Library, Greg Childs and BBC Record Breakers; Valerie Major and the Golden Hinde Book Shop, Bexhill Photographics, Second Spin, Bexhill. To my childhood teachers, my appreciation of their expertise, and of the teaching knowledge I subconsciously assimilated – in particular Marguerite Thomas, Enid Davies, Mrs Robert Davies, Gertrude Beaton, Joy Clarke and Shirley Weisbard. To the friends and acquaintants who gave their time to talk to me, sharing their knowledge and expertise, including Fred Strickler, Sam Weber, Jim Taylor, Dr Fayard Nicholas, Dr Leonard Reed, Dr Jeni LeGon, Joy Hewitt, Rusty Franks, Robert Reed, Fiona Castle and Hazel Banting; also to Joyce Percy, Daphne Peterson, Doreen Wells, Stanley Holden and Mary Clarke. To Douglas and Peggy Verral for kindly giving me helpful and constructive advice. For support and encouragement: Yvonne Durham, Jill Smith, Amanda Green, Caroline Lavelle, Anuschka Roes, Catherine Jameson, Rev Robin Rees, Elsa Rees, and to all the friends who encouraged me. To Rebecca for checking the photograph references, and Joshua for checking the index. To Daphne Sherry; to Myra Tiffin and Rosina; to Gaynor Walter, Ann Slacke and Roy Deutscher; to Liz Witt and Annette Clarke; to Jon Firth for his patience and photographic expertise.

All photographs in Part Two are by Jon Firth except where stated otherwise.

Front cover photograph: Grad Tap. Photograph by Jon Firth.

Back cover photograph: Rhapsody in Taps, Linda Sohl Donnel and Eddie Brown. Photograph by Philip Channing.

Every effort has been made to trace the owners of the copyright material used in this book, though in some cases these efforts were unsuccessful.

Typefaces used: Photina MT (main text); ITC Cheltenham Bold Condensed (headings).

Typeset and designed by
D & N Publishing, Hungerford, Berkshire.

Printed and bound in Great Britain by CPI Bath.

CONTENTS

FOREWORD

Heather Rees is an experienced and highly respected teacher with a clear and analytical approach. Not only will this informative book be a great asset to the dance teacher and student, but it will also be interesting for anyone who loves tap.

Joyce Percy (former examiner of classical ballet, modern theatre dance and tap dance, and chairman of the Imperial Society of Teachers of Dancing from 1991 to 2000).

INTRODUCTION

For those of you who have never embarked on this delightful form of recreation, I hope that reading this book will make your feet 'itch' to tread new ground, with flapping and scuffing and shuffling. And for those of you already dancing, or teaching, perhaps it will provide food for thought, some new ideas, and some variations on a theme. Take the ideas, use them, play around with them, change them, re-invent them, improve on them, make them your own. After all, dance, and particularly tap dancing, is in a world of plagiarism: but so is any art form. Modern music blatantly uses melodies and harmonies of the masters; artists are inspired to emulate great artists and entitle their paintings 'after Degas' or 'after Renoir'. Dramatists, too, have indulged in clever imitation: take as examples the conversion of *Romeo and Juliet* to *West Side Story*, or *Pygmalion* to *My Fair Lady* and later to *Educating Rita*.

There is an amusing story about Oscar Wilde. After hearing a very clever and humorous remark at a dinner party, he said, 'Oh! I wish *I'd* said that!' – to which one of his companions pertinently replied: 'You will, Oscar, you will!' There are similar amusing tales in the world of tap dance: for instance, Gregory Hines, after seeing Gene Kelly on screen, remarked that Mr Kelly had stolen some of his steps!

Tap history is full of diverse and talented dancers, and those who are carrying the torch and passing the art on to future generations value their contribution to its creative content.

ABOUT THE BOOK

This book is intended for teachers and student teachers. In part one there is a brief history of just some of the people and places responsible for the development of tap dancing, together with some information about floors and shoes. The music chapter, with its analysis of rhythm, also explains the method used for counting the sequences included in Part Two.

The second part contains a vocabulary of steps, then traditional steps and time steps, followed by some suggestions for using the steps. For easy reference the numbers are continuous, from the vocabulary at the beginning through to final sequences. There is a suggestion for a class plan, but the exercises can be chosen at random; thus they can be used as written, or adapted to suit your own requirements.

The music suggestions are also very flexible, and once the basic rhythm pattern has been established, there are many options available. Some of the sequences were specifically arranged to the particular track noted. However, they too can be adapted to suit other pieces of music if desired. The CD list contains a cross-section of types of music, including some that were written specifically for tap dancing or used in the heyday of tap dancing.

Tap is a dance form that can be enjoyed by a wide age range, from the very young child to the very mature adult. Thus, many people in their seventies and eighties are still tapping – it is fun and good exercise.

The appearance of Mr Fred Astaire is granted by a special licence from Mrs Astaire, Beverley Hills, California. All rights reserved.

1 A BRIEF HISTORY AND BACKGROUND

EARLY HISTORY

Tap dancing – a percussive rhythm achieved by clever manipulation of the feet – was born of the fusion of cultures on American soil. The African slaves took their innate rhythms with them when they were taken to America. During the voyage, recreation periods and entertainment sessions afforded the opportunity for the Africans and the British to view each other's form of rhythm and dance. The sailor's hornpipe, danced aboard ship, was originally a hard-shoe dance in which various mimetic gestures, imitating the jobs undertaken aboard ship, were combined with percussive foot sounds. Then in America the African population again met with clog dancing, and also with the step dancing of the Irish immigrants who were fleeing the potato famine in their native country. Gradually the blending of cultures and the exchange of ideas resulted in a new form of dance: tap dancing.

African Dancing and Foot Stomping

The African tribal dance was a flat-footed movement with bent knees, an upright carriage and a rhythmic impulse in the body. The drum rhythms were intricate and complex, and, unlike the rhythm of Western classical music, the Africans often gave equal importance to strong and weak beats. In 1739, when American law forbade the use of their native drums – even for dancing – they simply transferred their indigenous rhythms to their feet.

Clogging and Stepping

It was in the 1700s, with the founding of the cotton mills in the north of England during the Industrial Revolution, that the wearing of wooden-soled shoes amongst factory workers became widespread. The soles of these shoes were made from one solid piece of wood, and proved to be excellent protection from the conditions encountered by these workers. Thus wearing clogs became normal practice for the whole family, even the young children.

By the late eighteenth century, clog dancing was a well established art. The percussive rhythms of the clog dancers had reached high levels of expertise. Itinerant dancing masters travelled from town to town, hiring a barn or a kitchen to teach aspiring dancers; accommodation was given in exchange for lessons for the children of the host. The style required speed and energy, but the movement was from the hips down only: the arms were held rigidly at the sides, and the dance used little or no space.

In Ireland during the latter part of the eighteenth century, the dancing scene was similar. The dancing masters became part of the social scene, and it was they who shaped the future of Irish dancing, refining the performances and creating new steps and rhythms in both solo and step dancing. Their dances consisted of jigs, reels and hornpipes. (It is likely that the hornpipe originated in England in Elizabethan times, where it had been part of a stage act.)

In England, clog dancing continued to flourish throughout the 1800s. Competitions afforded an opportunity to display the expertise of the dancers, as well as providing a catalyst for the creation of new steps and rhythms. The action, however, was still contained in the footwork, the body retaining its original upright carriage. The Irish step dancing followed the same path, the most important aspect being the intricacy and rhythms of footwork, and the competitive element encouraging the creation of new steps. In both styles the body was erect and the arms held at the sides.

The Fusion

African native dancing, Irish step dancing and Lancashire clogging were the major ingredients of tap. The intricate and highly sophisticated African rhythms, combined with the shoe rhythms of the Europeans, were responsible for taking percussive dance to another dimension. However, it was the fundamental change in rhythm, with the introduction of syncopation, that was the influencing factor in the creation of tap dance.

From the mixing of these very different cultural backgrounds an exciting new dance form gradually emerged, and went on to develop with a variety and freedom of style. Tap, this ubiquitous form of dance, is now enjoyed by countless thousands of dancers, in varying degrees of expertise, all over the world.

The Dancers, the Dances and the Theatres

From its beginnings through to the present day, the growth and development of tap dance have been entirely due to the creative people who chose it as a career, and to the theatres, clubs, dance studios, film studios, street corners or side alleys that gave them the arena to perform. There were those who changed the footwork, the format or the phrasing, and others who introduced new and seemingly impossible actions in order to achieve the spectacular and to challenge records. All these people have a place in the history of tap dancing.

AMERICA: THE DANCE DEVELOPMENT

Minstrelsy and Minstrel Shows

Travelling shows were the original vehicle for spreading the work through the American continent; minstrelsy and minstrel shows were the early form of theatre. It is likely that there were two sources from which these shows evolved: one was white actors impersonating blacks, and the other was the black street musicians and singers who performed in the city streets.

One of the many travelling entertainers in the early days was Thomas Dartmouth Rice, a white entertainer who was credited with being the father of minstrelsy. In around 1828 he introduced a new routine comprising limping, shuffling and jigging movements, each phrase ending with a jump. He had been inspired by the shuffling movements of an elderly African stable hand whom he had watched in the stable behind the theatre. Rice blackened his face and danced the new-found 'shoe sounds' to the words of 'jump jim crow'; an oil painting showing the crowds surrounding him on stage bears testimony to his success, and this success marked the beginning of minstrel shows. The routine was popular in the United States and in Great Britain, where he introduced it in 1836, and many performers imitated his act. After the American Civil War, black entertainers – who, ironically, also often wore black make-up – became more prominent than previously.

Buck and Wing and Soft Shoe

In the latter part of the nineteenth century two types of dance routine became popular in the minstrel shows. One was the buck and wing, a fast dance performed in wooden-soled shoes, and the other was a soft-shoe dance for which leather shoes were worn. Harland and Dixon popularized the former, and George Primrose the latter.

The soft-shoe routine was slow, calm and elegant, originally danced in soft shoes and on sand. It was most certainly of African origin, using a development of African movements such as the 'Virginia essence'; later it was developed using tap shoes.

Buck and wing was a dance using a form of time-step and wings. It was performed in wooden-soled shoes, which, unlike the solid sole of the clog, were made with a split sole. The sound made with the maple-wood toe and heel was clean and crisp.

Metal Taps

Eventually it became popular to fix metal taps on the toes and heels of the shoes, and with this transition, a change in tone occurred. Most of the original dances performed in the theatres were of the repetitive kind. Thus a buck-and-wing dance would start with a time-step performed six times, followed by a two-bar break; the next step would also last for eight bars. Often a dancer would perform only four different steps in a dance. Flash steps such as wings and splits would comprise the concluding bars of the dance, and were intended to encourage applause. The soft-shoe dance consisted of various essences using a similar format of repeats and breaks.

Change of Rhythm

It was in the minstrel shows of the nineteenth century that popular music enjoyed the biggest exposure. Ragtime (influenced by the early banjo music) became popular, syncopation was introduced, and jazz music started its complex rhythmic development. Jigs, reels and hornpipes were rhythmically plain, repetitive and predictable, as were the marches from which ragtime emanated. The new style in music, with its unexpected accenting of off-beats, offered a much richer variety of rhythms, and tap dancers claim that they were instrumental in the development of the jazz rhythms. In extempore sessions with musicians, the tap dancers would often create rhythms with their feet, which were then taken up by the drummers, who in turn passed ideas back.

THE THEATRE

Vaudeville

Vaudeville as a family entertainment superseded the bawdier minstrel shows. In 1881 Tony Pastor doubled his audience potential in New York by offering shows that provided entertainment without vulgarity. However, although Pastor was the first to offer such entertainment, it was the Keith Circuit, opened in March 1894, that developed this concept on a large scale. Two entrepreneurs, Benjamin Franklyn Keith and Edward F. Albee, who joined him in 1857, were good businessmen who acquired a large number of theatres, their circuit eventually covering the area east of Chicago. The Orpheum Circuit managed by Martin Beck covered the area west of Chicago, and these two circuits provided constant work for a great number of artists, including the tap-dancing fraternity. The big theatres offered two shows a day up until the 1930s.

At the beginning of this period the famous clog dancer Pat Rooney, whose speciality was the waltz clog, is credited with popularizing 'the buffalo' and 'falling off the log'. Also George M. Cohan, a member of The Four Cohans, created an eccentric 'buck-and-wing' dance, which the audience loved. (Cohan was later immortalized by James Cagney in the film *Yankee Doodle Dandy*.)

The Role of Pickanninies

Pickanninies (often abbreviated to 'picks') were young black children who worked in white vaudeville. They were used to strengthen an otherwise weak show, and were expected to perform their song and dance act 'sensationally'. The pay was low, but for many young children, it was a good way to start a career.

Black Vaudeville

Black vaudeville existed in a separate dimension, and the two groups of entertainers did not mix during those times. Just prior to World War I a black comedian, Sherman Dudley, began leasing and purchasing theatres throughout the south and south-west specifically for his fellow artistes. The circuit was known as the 'Theater Owners' Booking Association' (T.O.B.A.), and it provided a starting point for many black artists, some of whom eventually became very well known.

The Lafayette Theater

The T.O.B.A. consisted of over forty-five theatres in the south and south-west, and there was another chain of theatres in the north-east specifically for black performers. The Lafayette Theater was one of these.

The Cotton Club

The famous Cotton Club was originally situated in the middle of Harlem and was a theatre for top black performers. Most of the well known jazz orchestras played there, as well as dancers, singers and comic acts. It opened in 1923, and in 1935 moved downtown to Broadway and 48th Street. However, although all the performers were black, their own friends were unable to watch them perform because the audience was for whites only.

Connie's Inn

Situated in Harlem, Connie's Inn was an exclusive club for black entertainers. In 1933 it was moved downtown.

DEVELOPMENTS IN THE TWENTIETH CENTURY

During the first half of the twentieth century there was an exponential growth in the number of tap dancers in theatre, and a rich development of the art. A plethora of productions existed in the many theatres throughout the United States, and every show had tap dancing, and most of them had several tap acts on the bill. Their names were as colourful and inventive as the acts they produced: there was flash tap, eccentric tap, legomania and class acts. Talented dancers in both the black and white community proliferated, many of them born of theatrical families. Often they became professionals while still young children, perhaps brothers, or brother and sister acts.

The Hoofers' Club

The Hoofers' Club must take much of the credit for this rapid development in the black community. The club was situated at the back of a poolroom two doors away from the Lafayette Theater on Seventh Avenue; the poolroom owner, Lonnie Hicks, enjoyed watching tap dancing, and he set the room aside for tap dancers. It was open twenty-four hours a day, and was never empty. There were probably twenty-five or thirty reputable dancing acts in the New York theatres at any one time, and many of the stars would spend time practising at the club; young novices were also encouraged to visit, and would creep in to watch and learn. Plagiarism was rife, the dancers watching each other closely to steal or trade steps, and the steps thus acquired would be modified or improved upon. However, all were aware of the one unwritten rule: 'Thou Shalt Not Copy Anyone's Steps – Exactly!'

To provide accompaniment, most dancers learned to play a theme on the rickety piano – just a single-note melody in crotchets, played with one finger in the style of stop-time. The more ambitious musicians would use a series of whole-note chords to accompany their tap-dancing friends and colleagues.

Street Dancers

Many youngsters practised their art on street corners or on the sidewalk, exchanging and developing ideas together. Dance was their main recreation, and many succeeded in their desire to become professional dancers.

In both the black and the white communities, those who reached great heights in the profession attained their high standards after long sessions practising (often alone in a studio for many hours) until they were satisfied with their level of perfection. Here again, competitions provided a desire to improve. In casual challenges on street corners or in formal competitions in theatres, dancers would vie with each other to prove their supremacy.

In the Theatres

In the theatres it was a golden age for tap dancing, and every show contained at least one tap-dance act – and most of them boasted many more. The names are numerous and colourful, such as Chuck and Chuckles, Buck and Bubbles, Pete, Peaches and Duke.

Repetitive Dances

Many dancers had only a small repertoire of dances. The shows they performed in would tour the theatres in America, and quite often a year would pass before they encountered the same audience again. Most of the dancers did an act that combined singing, dancing and telling jokes, and it was many years before tap dancing was considered an entertainment in its own right.

DANCERS AND DANCE FORMS

A rich tapestry of dancers existed from a variety of backgrounds. Whether performing, teaching or choreographing, these talented dancers learned their art by any means available to them and then developed, created and invented new foot movements, rhythms or phrases of sequences. All dancers contributed to the survival and progress of tap dancing, many of them innovators who effected definite changes in some particular aspect of tap. There was a complete set of white dancers as well as an enormous number of black entertainers, but all touring their own circuit and often unaware of any of the others. However, when they did meet, ideas would be exchanged and developed.

The Development of Irish Stepping

There are many examples of the integration of dance forms; James Barton's experience is one of these. A dancer who spent much of his career performing Irish step dancing, he was eventually to be influenced by the rhythms of the black dancers. He was of Irish descent, born in New Jersey in 1890, and was performing in the family act by the age of four. He could assimilate dance routines quickly, and he learned to develop the steps he copied from others.

Barton's style, with its roots in step dancing, involved the use of both toes and heels, whereas the Negro performers at that time used a flat-footed method of dancing. In the early days he had not seen a coloured dancer, and his sole inheritance was from Irish dancing. Later, when influenced by the rhythmic complexity of the Negros, he added more swing to his routines.

Flat-Footed African

King 'Rastus' Brown was probably the last of the flat-footed African dancers; his style of tapping had its roots in African gioube-stepping. His most famous dance was the 'Buck Dancer's Lament', consisting of six bars of time-step followed by an improvised break to two bars of stop-time.

Copasetics Club

In September 1949 the Copasetics Club was created in honour of Bill 'Bojangles' Robinson. During his long and successful career 'Bojangles' was one of the few black dancers who crossed the dividing line, performing in black and white vaudeville. He was, in the words of his goddaughter, '...one of the most accomplished, creative, famous and talented dancers' and '...his generosity to everyone, regardless of sex, race, creed or colour, will never be topped'.

Up From the Flat Foot

Bill 'Bojangles' Robinson was one of the innovators: he brought tap dancing away from the flat-footed Negro style up onto the toes, and this transition introduced a lightness into the quality of the tone. His shoes were of the wooden-soled variety, split along the instep. A buck dancer who used jigs and reels but not swing, his compositions consisted of eight-bar phrases, although he would sometimes ignore the break. He spent his career perfecting his act, rather than introducing new steps. His sequences were rhythmically interesting, his timing was exact, and his presentation exuded a certain indefinable charisma. According to Bill Bailey, who first saw him at The Lafayette in the late 1920s, Bill Robinson's performance was the 'prettiest thing' he had ever seen; and Nick Castle commented that 'Every tap was a pearl'. He started his career as a 'pickanniny' when he was twelve years old, and his career spanned decades; yet he did not become well known until he was in his fifties. Amongst other things he was famous for his stair-dance, a composition that maximized the use of various levels of tone. He is also remembered for some of his favourite expressions: 'I've never been so happy since I was coloured'; and 'Everything is Copasetic' meaning that it was 'better than okay'.

Toes and Heels

Another innovative dancer was John Bubbles. Although on his first visit to the Hoofers' Club he was a failure, later he made a major contribution to tap involving a change of footwork. As we have seen, Bill Robinson had taken tap away from flat-footed shuffling and up onto the toes; John Bubbles introduced the heels but not, as previously, in a flat-footed manner: instead he used the toe and heel separately, and this method increased the number of sounds possible within the measure. His work was partly influenced by some Lancashire clogging steps he had learned from another dance act as a child. He also introduced unusual accenting of off-beats and the use of greater dynamics of tone. Like Honi Coles, he worked for crisp clarity and tone quality in the use of both the heels and the balls of the feet.

THE INFLUENCE OF INDIVIDUAL STYLES

Eddie Rector was an influence and mentor to many young dancers. His dancing was the exception to rhythmic monotony: he invented new combinations, and his dancing was characterized by elegance of motion as he made use of all the available stage area.

Leonard Reed and **Willie Bryant** were responsible for the creation of the Shim Sham Shimmy, which has now become the national anthem of tap dancing. Being of mixed parentage, for many years they were able to perform undetected in both white and black vaudeville.

Family Acts

During the time of vaudeville there were many family acts, with two, three or four members, as well as friends working together, sometimes pretending to be brothers. Some of the well known names in this period were the Four Covans, the Whitman Sisters, the Berry Brothers, the Step Brothers, Pete and Peaches, Chuck and Chuckles, Reed and Bryant, Buck and Bubbles, to name but a few.

The **Whitman Sisters** were responsible for nurturing the talent of many young dancers who later became stars.

The **Four Covans** danced on the Orpheum Circuit and the Keith Circuit. Willie Covan, the most

The Ziegfeld Follies

After an opening performance in July 1907, on a small garden stage at the top of a New York Theatre, the Ziegfeld Follies ran for almost twenty-three years. The extravaganza of dancing, music and comedy, with its troupes of beautiful girls (sometimes as many as sixty or seventy-five), was the creation of the young Florenz Ziegfeld (son of Dr Florenz Ziegfeld, president of the Chicago Musical College). Inspired by the Folies Bergères, his (less infamous) version became a phenomenon of show business, and ensured him a place in theatrical history.

talented of the group, had spent his life tap dancing, and his love of rhythm had been fed by the 'clickety-click' sound of streetcars. He had started work as a 'pickanniny' when he was six years old.

Chorus Lines

There were very few female solo acts, and most girl dancers found work in chorus lines such as the Cotton Club Girls, The Reedettes, and the Zeigfeld Follies. They performed precision work of tap dancing and high kicking, and some of the girls did 'toe dancing', which involved tapping 'on pointe'. There were also chorus lines of boys, or of mixed boys and girls.

A Faster Tap

Honi Coles and **Cholly Atkins** were a tall and elegant class act. Honi Coles developed further the fast tapping of John Bubbles; he was also one of the first dancers to extend the phrase beyond eight counts. Coles grew up in Philadelphia where tap was extremely popular. He started his career in a trio, but when the act broke up he spent a whole year practising in his room for twelve to fourteen hours a day, and finally emerged with the fastest feet in the business. Cholly Atkins describes him as being 'the creator of high-speed rhythm tap', saying that his tapping was faster than Bubbles. Coles described Atkins as being a more modern dancer than the remainder of the group.

They became famous for their incredibly slow, controlled and highly polished performance of the soft-shoe dance. The choreography of the piece was rhythmically clever and inventive, but retained the traditional style. They moved in exact unison with each other, and this was a joy to watch. Honi Coles is also remembered for his own arrangement of 'The Walk Around', a piece containing a clever combination of riffs and riff walks. It is ironic that someone with such dextrous and rapid footwork should be famous for slow pieces.

Improvisation

Laurence Jackson was known professionally as 'Baby' Laurence: at eleven years old he was singing with the John Redman band. His biggest thrill was his first visit to the Hoofers' Club in New York.

Whilst touring, his inspiration had come from studying the acts of Pete, Peaches and Duke, as well as Bill Bailey and Derby Wilson. At the Hoofers' Club his mentors were people such as Eddie Rector and Harold Mablin. Like so many other dancers, he had been helped by Leonard Reed in the forming of his act, and had worked with bands such as that of Duke Ellington, Count Basie, and Woodie Herman. His knowledge of the standard steps was sound, but his performances were based on improvisation, with the scattered inclusion of fragments of the well known steps. As a finale in the last days of the Hoofers' Club he improvised a 'Concerto in Percussion'. His concentration on footwork, its clarity, and the complexity of sounds and rhythm, marked the beginning of yet another phase in the history of tap dancing.

Dancing with a Peg Leg

Peg Leg Bates achieved the seemingly impossible. At twelve years old he commenced work in a cotton mill, and tragically lost a leg in an accident with a conveyor belt; it was amputated just below the knee, and a peg leg was fitted. The loss did not affect his desire to dance, and by the time he was fifteen years old he had established a very successful career. The rhythms of his peg leg equalled those of his good foot, and his ability to tap and perform flash steps was undiminished by the potential handicap; his career took him to top venues such as The Cotton Club and Connie's Inn.

AMERICAN INFLUENCE IN BRITAIN

Meanwhile, in Britain the dance scene had not been dormant. During the latter part of the nineteenth and the beginning of the twentieth century the influence of the American theatre was evident in the music halls (the equivalent of the American vaudeville), when minstrelsy and minstrel shows became popular.

Throughout the history of tap dancing, Britain has been influenced by the American development. Theatrical acts constantly toured between the two countries: thus British dancers who travelled to America would return with new inspiration, and American dancers visiting Britain similarly influenced British dancers. Many Americans made their home in Britain, passing on their art to those who were eager to learn.

Music Hall and Minstrel Shows

The Great Mackney, born in 1823, was one of the early 'black-up' artists; but probably the most famous of the minstrels was Eugene Stratton. Billed as 'The Dandy Coloured Coon', Stratton was an American who came to England with a minstrel show in the latter part of the 1880s. He stayed in Britain to become one of its best loved variety performers, and in 1912 was nominated for the first Royal Command Performance.

His songs were acted rather than sung, and he excelled at the soft-shoe dance, drifting into soft-shoe steps at the end of his song. Stratton's graceful style proved to be a great influence on Jack Buchanan, who in later years emulated his soft-shoe dance almost exactly. Another 'magical minstrel' performer in music hall was George H. Elliot, who, according to Mr Will Bishop, was 'no mean performer of the soft-shoe dance'.

THE DANCE SCENE IN BRITAIN

Clog Dancing

Highly developed clog-dancing acts were already firmly established in the music halls. Charlie Chaplin was a clog dancer who toured the music halls with a group called 'The Lancashire Lads'. One of the most famous acts in the second half of the nineteenth century was champion clog dancer Dan Leno, born in a trunk in 1861 and 'on the boards' while still very young. In 1883 he won an impressively engraved silver-buckled belt declaring him 'The Champion Clog Dancer of the World'. He was also one of the most famous pantomime dames.

Pantomime

Pantomime has been a popular form of entertainment since the nineteenth century. The comedy scripts, loosely based on one of the well known fairy tales, consisted of a standard format of characters, and many productions had as many as twenty-four chorus girls to enact the crowd scenes. Part of the chorus would be made up of a

The 1930s Tiller Girls: 'Off To Hollywood'. (Courtesy of Doremy Vernon)

speciality act who were provided with a slot – usually near the end of the show – to present their precision routine of tap dancing and high kicking. The routines were similar to those of the Cotton Club Girls and other troupes who were touring the American theatres.

John Tiller and the Tiller Girls

In the early 1880s the famous John Tiller started his long association with the theatre. He became a stage manager, and was responsible for an amateur group called the Minnehaha Minstrels: their faces blackened with burnt cork, they performed in the Manchester theatres, raising money for charity.

In 1885 Tiller began teaching dance to children, and by 1890 he presented a group of four little girls in a Manchester pantomime. From these small beginnings he went on to become world famous. He would rehearse every movement of the group until they were exhausted and their feet were sore – but the result was a troupe in perfect unison. The Tiller Girls – a tap-dancing, high-kicking, precision troupe of dancers – became world famous, their tours taking them to many exciting venues, including Hollywood.

From Clogging to Tapping

The Four Ascots

Clog-dancing acts were still performing at the beginning of the twentieth century. One excellent act was known as the 'Four Ascots', famous on the music hall circuit: two sisters – champion clog dancers from the North of England – had met two Australian brothers, and together they formed a clog-dancing act. When they were at their most famous, they met some American dancers who had metal taps on the soles of ordinary dancing shoes; at this time they also encountered the 'new' jazz music. This prompted them to exchange the clogs for tap shoes, and to use the sounds and syncopated rhythms of the new music. The decision probably resulted in them being the first jazz tap dancers in England.

Their repertoire included routines to Alexander's Rag-Time Band and Scott Joplin-type music; they also choreographed a marvellous 'Tango Tap' using authentic tango steps overlaid with the sound of taps. During their career they toured empires, hippodromes and palaces throughout England, performed at the 'number one' theatres in Europe, and undertook long tours of South Africa and Australia. Very often such was the length and enthusiasm of their ovation that they would have to return to the stage after reaching their dressing rooms. And there was one momentous occasion when the speed of their dancing confounded the orchestra at the London Palladium: they completed their dance with drum alone.

The group split up at the outbreak of World War I, but after the war Dougie Ascot opened a studio in Charing Cross Road. There he taught many famous people, including Jack Hulbert, Sally Gray, Dickie Henderson and eventually his own daughter Hazel. The young Hazel Ascot was featured in films at the same time as Shirley Temple. Although the British dance films did not achieve the fame of the American ones, young Hazel's speed and clarity in her tap dancing was a credit to her father's teaching.

The Sherry Brothers
At the start of World War I the Sherry Brothers, who had been taught by their father, entered show business with a clog-dancing act. Their family roots in show business were well established, and clog dancing was, in those days, a normal act in the

The Five Sherry Brothers who became a tap-dancing act, in the early 1900s, after meeting some American tap dancers. (Courtesy Daphne Sherry)

music hall. However, after meeting some visiting American tap dancers, they decided to become a tap-dancing act. Calling themselves The Five Sherry Brothers, they received great acclaim with their opening show in the Empire London, after which they toured all over the country.

Tap dancing continued to gain popularity in Britain, and in the twenties the exchanges of visits between American and British dancers furthered the culture.

BRITISH THEATRE

At the end of the nineteenth and the beginning of the twentieth century the theatre circuit in Britain was vast. As on the American circuit, there were different levels of theatre, providing work for well known stars as well as for the less experienced and less famous; the empires and hippodromes, and the music halls and workingmen's clubs were host to a multitude of variety artists – and the dream of every one of them was eventually to appear in the West End.

Jack Buchanan

One West End theatre owner was Jack Buchanan, known as the greatest song-and-dance man. In 1911 he started a career that spanned over forty years; his forte was the soft-shoe dance, at which he excelled. Almost entirely self-taught, he had, like so many dancers, learned from watching great performers in the West End. His admiration for Eugene Stratton continued with him into his own very successful career, and he used his idol's style of soft-shoe dance for his first audition. In later years the soft-shoe dance he performed after the song 'And Her Mother Came Too' was one of the favourites of the then Prince of Wales.

More Chorus Troupes

In the first half of the twentieth century there were many troupes of dancers emulating the Tiller Girls. Some achieved fame and recognition; others eventually dissolved into oblivion. One of the eminently successful groups of dancers was created by a young Irish girl from Dublin: her name was Margaret Kelly. She became known as 'Bluebell' because of a chance remark made by a general practitioner about her clear blue eyes.

At fourteen she danced with a Scottish party, and within less than a year became a 'Jackson Girl'. In that precision-dancing troupe of thirty girls she performed in Berlin and in Paris until economic problems resulted in a temporary lull. She returned to London hoping to obtain work with Jack Buchanan at his newly opened Leicester Square Theatre. However, another offer took her back to Paris, this time with the J.W. Jackson Girls, and from there she eventually started her own troupe, calling them the 'Bluebell Girls'.

They opened in November 1932 at the Folies Bergères, and by December 1933 were part of the cine-variety shows (based on that of Radio City Music Hall in New York). Originally eleven girls, the number was increased to twenty-four, and they provided the stunning opening item, following an introductory orchestral suite. Throughout a highly successful career her girls became world famous. Their home was in Paris, but their world-wide tours included performing in Las Vegas.

Other successful troupes were Sherman Fishers (one of their numbers was a military-style dance), J.W. Jackson's (who performed a very clever fast tap dance imitating the sound of a train), and the Doreen Austin Girls (whose sailor dance had been costumed by a professional 'Navy tailor'). There were many of these 'theme' dances, and – like the steps for buck-and-wing and soft shoe – they contained specific combinations that became traditional, and were passed on to successive generations.

Most of these troupes are now part of history. The Bluebell Girls and the Tiller Girls survived the longest.

AMERICANS IN ENGLAND

There were many Americans dancers who came to Britain and decided to stay.

Buddy Bradley
Bradley was born in Pennsylvania; he was a product of American tap dancing. His sojourn in London was to influence the course of tap dancing. He taught dance techniques to many Broadway and West End stars of the 1920s and 1930s.

In his home country he had learned by watching people like Dancing Dotson and Jack Wiggins at the local theatre in Harrisburg, although his preference was for the assortment of Afro-American steps such as the charleston, the strut, the drag and the shuffle. By the time he was fourteen he had lost both his parents; after a short spell living with his brother-in-law, he moved to New York City. The boarding house at which he resided was also home to show-business people, many of whom were dancers.

In between working as an elevator boy, he practised in the blind alley next to Connie's Inn. Initially the competition at the Hoofers' Club was too fast for him, although later he progressed sufficiently to become part of that scene. He learned wings, flips, knee-drops and many more acrobatic steps, and he danced in the Connie's Inn chorus, but eventually had an opportunity to choreograph solos. However, he soon tired of the monotonous repetition of steps and rhythms that were prevalent amongst the dancers. Even so, in his opinion Bill 'Bojangles' Robinson could make the simplest rhythms look great, and Eddie Rector, with his inventive combinations and use of space, was inspirational to Bradley's already fertile imagination. Bradley's talent for interpreting rhythms and improvising jazz music into dance patterns was new to Broadway. Generally he ignored the melody and concentrated on following the accent of the soloist.

He welcomed the opportunity to work in London, choreographing for Charles B. Cochran, known as the Zeigfeld of England, where he was responsible for sixty-four dancers, including sixteen Tiller Girls.

Bradley also successfully choreographed for very many films, although his only appearance on the screen was in *Evergreen* (1934). He worked in collaboration with Jessie Matthews on a number of films, and his choreography for her performance of 'Dancing on the Ceiling' was memorable.

After World War II he ran his own dancing school in London's West End, and amongst the dancers who attended his classes were stars such as Sir John Mills, Jack Buchanan and Bruce Forsyth.

The Condos Brothers
In 1932 the Condos brothers, Frank and Nick, toured Europe. In Paris they received a mixed reaction: the French liked their eccentric dance and body movements, but they showed little understanding of

Sony Hale rehearsing the Buddy Bradley Girls for Evergreen. (Evergreen *courtesy of Carlton International Ltd. LFI.)*

tap dancing. Then the brothers accepted a booking for two weeks at the London Palladium – and stayed for two years. Their act consisted of a soft-shoe number as well as wings. The wing had begun to develop at the beginning of the 1900s, and by the 1920s most dancers were performing three-tap wings. A variety of wings developed by the 1930s, but Frank Condos eventually achieved an exceptional five-tap wing (the five sounds being executed with one foot), which he also taught his brother. However, they eventually dropped the complicated wings from their act.

They returned to America, and after eight years together the younger brother, Steve, replaced Frank. **Steve Condos** was renowned for his ability to produce spontaneous improvisation. This talent for rhythm rapport emanated from his childhood friendship with the jazz drummer Buddy Rich, and

the influence of trumpet player Louis Armstrong. In fact his improvisational skills were so secure that Gower Champion allowed him to ad lib in performance, hitherto unheard of in a Broadway show. An avid and enthusiastic tapper, he was constantly creating and sharing rhythms (often a cappella), and he travelled the world teaching and performing in workshops.

CLASSICAL INFLUENCE ON TAP

Paul Draper's contribution to the world of tap is documented in the many articles written by and about him, and also in the book he wrote on the subject of tap dancing. He is respected and remembered in America and Britain for his classical style and his analytical approach. Born in Italy of American parents, his dance training was undertaken as a mature student. His musical parents introduced him to classical music at a very young age, and this influenced him in later years when he was trying to find his niche.

When the Drapers returned to America it was intended that Paul should train to become a civil engineer. However, frustrated with a desire to express himself, he took tap-dancing lessons on Broadway for 50 cents a lesson.

In 1931, in the jazz era, he enjoyed the music of Duke Ellington, particularly the Mooch and Black and Tan Fantasy, and perfected a time-step to this type of music. At that time his style lacked finesse, but nevertheless he set sail for England with a collection of gramophone records and some letters of introduction. Although he met up with, and was assisted by, all the right people, his lack of training resulted in an ignominious start in theatre.

He returned to America, and with some newly worked-out rhythms, performed a pedestal dance; but sadly he realized that he had not found what he wanted. He hit on the idea of dancing to the classical music with which he was so familiar. He took ballet lessons with Balanchine in order to strengthen his overall technique and improve his style. With the success that followed the perfecting of his art, he danced with symphony orchestras all over the world as well as in concert halls, music halls and movies. For many years he danced to the accompaniment of Larry Adler's harmonica. He performed and taught in London, and in Warner Brothers' *Colleen* he accompanied the lovely Ruby Keeler.

HOLLYWOOD AND FILMS

In the early 1930s, 'sound' movies tolled the death knell for vaudeville and for many of the vaudeville acts, and many tap-dance acts also found themselves out of work. Those who made the transition to the movie industry were lucky, and there was also

Paul Draper and Ruby Keeler in Colleen. *(Colleen © 1936 Turner Entertainment Co. An A.O.L. Time Warner Company. All rights reserved.)*

20

a new young generation of tap dancers whose careers blossomed in the world of celluloid: cinema offered a new and bigger opportunity for tap dancing to be broadcast around the world. In the early stages of cinema the programmes were padded out with live shows. This enabled many of the vaudeville acts to continue working, and there was always a tap-dancing act included.

Spreading the Word

Sadly, the films did not feature all the clever dancers. The number of expert dancers used compared to those available was minimal – and this was particularly true of the black dancers. However, the film industry reached out to a wider audience with a resulting increase in the number of tap devotees. The stars of the screen were an inspiration to hundreds of young hopefuls all over the world. Amongst the most well known were tap dancers such as Fred Astaire, Ginger Rogers, Eleanor Powell, Ann Miller, Gene Kelly, Bill 'Bojangles' Robinson, Shirley Temple, the Nicholas brothers, Jeni LeGon, Donald O'Connor, Gene Nelson, the Condos brothers, and Sammy Davis Junior.

New Developments

The lavish films with spectacular sets were the background for new, exciting and inventive choreographies. The structure of the routines became less repetitive. This element had already shown itself in live theatre, but on films the necessity for new work in each film was essential. Clever use of the linking of the steps, the phrasing of the sequences, the subtle use of syncopation and cross-phrasing was evident as new ideas were passed between choreographer and dancer. Props were incorporated into the highly polished routines in a way that blended into the movements and the story line. The elegant top hat with the cane (reminiscent of vaudeville), the umbrella in *Singin' In the Rain*, dustbin lids in *It's Always Fair Weather*, a clothes tree in *Royal Wedding*, and swinging on a chandelier in *Silk Stockings* were all used to great effect.

There was extensive use of chorus girls and chorines, from small groups through to a hundred Zeigfeld Follies, all dancing in unison. The disciplined rehearsals necessary to achieve unanimity of performance is much more exacting for films than for theatre: in theatre a slight disparity of leg or arm line can pass unnoticed; the camera is less forgiving.

THE STARS

Fred Astaire

The most prolific series of films made were those of Fred Astaire. When Astaire went to Hollywood he was already a very experienced performer, since at thirty-four years of age his career had already spanned twenty-eight years. The ease and grace of his movements, and the elegance and the flawlessness of his performances were legendary, and his style of dancing was unique.

His professional career with his sister Adele was launched on vaudeville at the age of six. In 1916 they went into Broadway musicals. He was beginning to earn a reputation as a tap dancer when in 1928, at a buck-dancing contest, he tied for third place with Will Mahoney. Bill Robinson and Jack Donoghue won first and second.

In the early twenties Fred and Adele Astaire visited England, first touring and then in London; their London debut was an unqualified success. Whilst he was there, Fred saw and was impressed by the style and elegance of Jack Buchanan; many years later they featured in a film together.

The Astaires returned to Broadway, and when Adele retired on her marriage, Fred went to Hollywood. In this new and extremely successful era of his career he danced with many partners in over thirty films; Audrey Hepburn expressed the sentiments of many female dancers when she said how wonderful it was '...to just once ... dance ... with Fred Astaire'.

In his choreography he drew on his own experience, and from working with such dance directors and choreographers as Hermes Pan and Nick Castle. Before his films he rehearsed for hours, striving for perfection, and as his career progressed he became more and more of a perfectionist.

Ginger Rogers

In Ginger Rogers he had a partner whose sympathetic performance provided a long and enduring partnership. Her moves matched his exactly, and they blended to perfection. Her own career began

21

when she won a competition dancing the charleston. In a glamorous Hollywood career she made seventy-three films, of which ten were with Fred Astaire. Later she developed her own night-club act, with four male dancers. In nostalgic performances, partnered by the elegant and talented Jim Taylor, she re-created many of the numbers she had performed with Fred Astaire.

Eleanor Powell also partnered Fred Astaire, and she provided a bigger challenge technically. She had a positive style of her own, and was a brilliant tapper.

Ann Miller is another unforgettable tap dancer, with taps that rattled to machine-gun proportions, and legs insured for a million dollars.

Gene Kelly

Gene Kelly started out in vaudeville as one of the Five Kellys. Later, when his parents took over a dancing school, he was an extremely popular instructor. His long career in films resulted in box office successes such as *On The Town* and *An American in Paris*. He danced with many different partners, but perhaps his favourite was the partnership with Tom and Jerry.

Singin' in the Rain is the film that best illustrates the birth of sound films and is partly a parallel of Gene Kelly's own career. In it he played the part of a vaudevillian who had risen to the heights of matinée idol. In his dance set to the title song his sense of joy and humour were infectious. Swinging around a lamp-post and splashing through puddles, umbrella in hand, he has inspired professional as well as the most timid of amateur dancers to attempt imitation – including Morecambe and Wise.

The Nicholas Brothers

The amazing Nicholas Brothers worked between vaudeville and Hollywood. Born into a theatrical family, they grew up surrounded by exceptional talent. Their parents, who had their own orchestra, played at the Standard Theater in Philadelphia. From an early age Fayard sat in the auditorium watching rehearsals, or stood in the wings during a performance, and so learned his art from such connoisseurs as Eddie Rector, the Berry Brothers, Peg Leg Bates, Slow Kid Thompson and Arthur Bryson. In 1929 he saw Willie Covan, of the Four Covans,

Gene Kelly dancing with Tom and Jerry. (Anchors Aweigh © 1945 Turner Entertainment Co. An A.O.L. Time Warner Company. All rights reserved.)

dancing acrobatic and soft shoe. Leonard Reed was to prove one of the greatest influences on the Nicholas Brothers. Reed, who had teamed up with Willie Bryant, moved with style and grace, and theirs was a classy, well-dressed act.

Fayard often practised barefoot, improvising without music, but he liked the sound of hard-soled street shoes. When he failed to interest his sister Dorothy in his enthusiasm for tap dancing, he tried his younger brother. Harold, who was a precocious child and a clever mimic, shared Fayard's love of dance. Soon, to the amazement their parents, the children had put together a routine without music. Their first public appearance was actually on a radio show, for which Fayard acquired his first pair of tap shoes.

Recognizing the special talent of the boys, their parents wisely steered them into a professional career, rather than attending competitions and amateur talent performances. They worked at The Lafayette in New York, and for most of the thirties they appeared at The Cotton Club. Their professional career spanned more than sixty years, in which

The Nicholas Brothers in Stormy Weather. *(Stormy Weather ©1943 Twentieth Century Fox. All rights reserved.)*

time they made six films for Twentieth Century Fox, performed on Broadway in Ziegfeld Follies, and then made their first trip to England to star in the London production of 'Black Birds of 1936.'

They dressed immaculately, and their dancing was magic. They called it classical tap: a combination of athleticism with tap dance, graceful body movements and artistic use of hands. These attributes, together with personalities that exuded the sheer joy of performing, made theirs a unique act. This talent was clearly evident in their performance of 'To Be a Clown' with Gene Kelly; but their most memorable performance is the stupendous routine in the Twentieth-Century Fox film *Stormy Weather*. Their fast-paced tap; their flying leaps over one another descending a flight of

stairs; their rhythmical, sensitive spring back up the stairs into the final sliding splits down the two symmetrical ramps, was (and is) unequalled. The energy and exuberance of this polished performance continued through their bow and exit.

Theirs was an act that displayed professionalism and maturity from a very early age. Their ability was unique, and their presence, energy, polish and class, whether singing, dancing or speaking, was unequalled.

Bill 'Bojangles' Robinson

Robinson's career enjoyed a new lease of life in Hollywood films. His famous staircase dance was successfully adapted as a duet with the delightful Shirley Temple in *The Little Colonel*. In a series of films with

Shirley Temple dancing with Bill 'Bojangles' Robinson. Shirley had already made five films, starting in 1934, before being cast with 'Bojangles' in The Little Colonel. *It was decided to adapt his stair dance on the grand staircase of the old colonial mansion in which the film was set, and to use Shirley for part of it. He taught her to keep her steps small and precise and, once the steps were mastered, she used maximum concentration to rehearse and polish the routine. The stair dance was the highlight of the film. (*The Little Colonel *©1935 Twentieth Century Fox. All rights reserved.)*

the young Shirley he found her quick to learn and a joy to partner. The films of Shirley Temple were sold out as soon as they were advertised. Aspiring parents took their young offspring to dancing lessons in the hope of emulating her success, and the dance studios were assured of increased patronage with each new release.

Jeni LeGon

Dancing with the bubbling and vivacious Jeni LeGon in *Hooray for Love* gave Bill Robinson an opportunity to dance with a partner of more maturity. As a young child Jeni knew that she wanted to dance, and in a career lasting over seventy years she danced in Hollywood, New York, London and Europe, in films, on stage and on television. In between she followed a teaching career, passing on the joy of dance to many. Her students credit her with the ability to recognize their weaknesses and strengths, and to turn them all to positive account. A lifetime's experience coupled with compassion, sensitivity and strong discipline are the ingredients of her recipe for success.

At ten years old she would gather the local children together and, using only the best of them, produce concerts for the neighbours. The audience used the external stairways leading to the apartments, and the children performed on the sidewalk, dancing to the music of improvised instruments. Street dancing was her learning process. Her inspiration was watching the dancers in the live performances, which in those days accompanied the showing of movies. There was always a tap-dancing act, which she would watch, carefully assimilating their steps; and after practising, she would return to check for accuracy, her final aim being to produce something more impressive.

The first time she auditioned professionally was the moment she established the desire to dance in trousers. Nevertheless, although she continued to perform in such attire regularly throughout her career, she could look equally stunning in the most feminine and glamorous of costumes.

Jeni's performances were unique in that she was probably the only female dancer to attempt – and with success – all the flash steps usually performed by the men. Her high jumps, and her performance of the splits with controlled recovery, were second to none. Her tap dancing was rhythmic and rippling, and in addition she was a competent toe dancer.

In the early days she joined the famous Whitman Sisters, whose organization in Chicago presented a complete black revue of jazz band and dancers.

Bill 'Bojangles' Robinson dancing with Jeni LeGon in Hooray for Love. *Inset is Fats Waller. (Hooray for Love © Turner Entertainment Company. An A.O.L. Time Warner Company. All rights reserved.)*

They were strict, but it was a good training ground. Later, teaming up with her foster sister, they took their act to Hollywood – and that was when she successfully auditioned for a film to partner the great Bill 'Bojangles' Robinson: his only ever grown-up partner. Their duets were a feat of rhythmic clarity and bubbling presentation, and they were entertaining right through to their last exit.

Visit to Britain

England had the pleasure of seeing her vibrant performances when C.B. Cochran – considered to be the Ziegfield of England – featured her in *Follow the Sun* at the Adelphi Theatre in 1936. The critics acclaimed her as the second Florence Mills, but qualified it by saying, 'she has a distinctive charm of her own'. (One of the children in the show was a very young Sarah Churchill.)

That extra little indefinable quality that makes star quality was ever present in Jeni's performances, whether stage or screen. Whoever else was dancing, one's eyes were drawn to her, and her ability to 'sell' a number is a quality she has passed on to her many students. Introduced to the Hoofers' Club at the time of John Bubbles, she became one of the few female members in that legendary room, rich with the atmosphere of the talented and famous foot percussionists.

Settled in Vancouver, her energy and vitality have not diminished. This tapping legend, now in her early eighties, is still teaching and performing, and at the time of writing is planning to travel the world!

Young Stars

There was another, less well known part of the film world in which many young talented dancers forged their tap-dancing careers. Universal Pictures made a series of films, one of which featured a group of young dancers, calling them 'The Jivin' Jacks and Jills': Roland Dupree, Peggy Ryan and Bob Scheerer were three of the twelve dancers, and were already talented tappers and soloists. Donald O'Connor, less experienced though quick to learn, had been a performer with his family in a circus act; he was less prepared for the speed and dexterity of footwork that had to be assimilated and polished quickly for the making of the films. Louis Dapron, a very clever teacher and choreographer, was instrumental in helping him through this period.

Bob Scheerer was already a successful dancer, and he was thirteen years old when he was put under contract to Universal. His impressive solo performances contained rippling, rhythmic footwork, fast, well controlled turns, and a performance full of energy and vitality. His career took him to Broadway, where at nineteen he worked with Gower Champion,

Jeni LeGon in C.B. Cochran's Follow The Sun *1935–36. (Courtesy of Dr Jeni LeGon)*

and at twenty-eight was in the Broadway production of *The Boy Friend* with Julie Andrews.

TEACHERS AND CHOREOGRAPHERS

Throughout this, the golden age of tap dancing, the many clever teachers and choreographers worked behind the scenes coaching young stars and arranging some of their routines. Hermes Pan worked with Fred and Ginger, and often dubbed the taps for Ginger Rogers when she was away making other films. Some of the most notable choreographies of Nick Castle were created for the Nicholas Brothers. Louis Dapron's excellent teaching aided the success of stars such as Donald O'Connor, as well as being instrumental in training other young stars. Henry LeTang worked endlessly with young hopefuls, including the now famous Gregory Hines.

Dance Schools

Dance schools were mainly responsible for spreading the work in all parts of the world. In Britain these included boarding and professional training schools; amongst the oldest of these were Cone-Ripman (now Arts Educational Schools) and Bush Davies.

The Jivin' Jacks and Jills: left to right: Corky Geil, Dottie Babb, Roland Dupree, McNobb, Donald O'Connor, McNabb, Tommy Rall, unidentified, Robert Scheerer. (Courtesy of Robert Scheerer)

Bush Davies Schools

Bush Davies (1914–89), one of England's most famous and prestigious schools, provided the training ground for a multitude of successful dancers who went into theatre and films, or became teachers and then examiners. Founded by Pauline Bush, it was later under the directorship of her daughter Noreen Bush, a meticulous and dedicated teacher, and Marjorie Davies, a gifted teacher whose appreciation of individual talents was a valuable asset in steering pupils into a suitable career. After a successful career in theatre, Victor Leopold also joined the Board of Directors. His methodical and thorough teaching of the rudiments of tap produced competent exponents of the art.

There were two young students who, to the chagrin of the directors, habitually broke the dawn silence with their early morning practising of tapdance. When they grew up, Joyce Percy and Daphne Peterson became the most dedicated of teachers; they eventually became directors.

The school produced some of the theatrical profession's most talented dancers. Stanley Holden, a protégé of Bush Davies, had reason to be grateful for his tap-dance training when playing the part of Widow Simone in the Royal Ballet Company's *La Fille Mal Gardée* in 1960. Frederick Ashton based his choreography for the dance on traditional Lancashire clogging. However, Stanley also made a contribution when he used one of Victor Leopold's tap steps as one

Stanley Holden dancing the clog dance of Widow Simone in La Fille Mal Gardée. *(Photograph by Houston Rogers)*

In 1989 Bush Davies School closed. A Tribute to Bush Davies was performed by many past students. The photograph shows Philip Gould and Doreen Wells rehearsing for their part in the production. Philip Gould played the lead in the West End production of 42nd Street. (Harry Drewett)

of the breaks. It was Stanley's exceptional talent for tap dancing (he won a Junior Championship in the Sunshine Competitions) that first introduced him to full-time training where he studied classical dance, and eventually forged a successful career, commencing in the Sadlers' Wells Royal Ballet Company.

Another graduate, the exquisite Doreen Wells, whose excellence in classical ballet was matched by her ability to tap dance and to perform in musical theatre, started her career with The Royal Ballet Company. Later, when playing leading roles in musical theatre, she always looked for an opportunity to tap.

EXAMINATIONS AND COMPETITIONS

Examinations are a major part of the dance scene in Britain. Many societies were formed in the early part of the twentieth century. Some faded away whilst others became stronger. The Imperial Society of Teachers of Dancing (founded in 1904) survived to become one of the biggest, encompassing many different forms of dance. Tap was first introduced in 1932, with the forming of the Stage Branch (later to become the Modern Theatre Dance Faculty). Zelia Raye was instrumental in formulating the original syllabus. During her many visits to America she was impressed with the all-round training of the Americans. She studied modern and tap dance (together with Joan Davis), and introduced the work to the Imperial Society. During the succeeding years Moyra Gay made a major impact on its development, with input from Tom Parry, Doreen Austin, Daphne Peterson, Gwen Carter, Marianne Jepson and others. In the 1980s and early 1990s there was a completely new approach, with a revision of the tap grades and major syllabi undertaken by Gwen Carter, Patricia Ellis and the author. Daphne Peterson and Sheelagh Harbinson were also involved at major level.

Other Societies

Several other examining bodies conduct tap examinations, one of which, the British Ballet Organization (founded in 1930), has a syllabus for children, students and teachers. Deborah Clark and Jurek Stroka created their revised syllabus.

Sunshine Competitions

Competitions have always been part of the dance scene, and the Sunshine Competitions, founded in the early 1920s, were popular throughout Britain. They provided a challenge and experience for young dancers, and the proceeds were donated to blind babies. In 1960 they were taken over by the 'All England' and registered as a charity.

IN SUMMARY

During its gradual evolution, tap dance has been developed, by imitation and plagiarism coupled with creative ability and talented invention, to a degree of incredible complexity and artistry that could not have been envisaged by its early exponents. The styles are as varied and interesting as the proliferation of steps and rhythms that have appeared as a result of its spread.

A second requiem for tap dancing occurred when the film *Oklahoma* was made. This film, with Agnes de Milne as its choreographer, turned to modern dance to help tell its story. Ensuing films followed its example, and tap dancers were no longer in vogue.

2 RENAISSANCE AND NOW

Many people believe that tap died in the era after the filming of *Oklahoma*; however, this assumption is not strictly true. Tap may have lost its arena in the theatres and in films, but it was 'simmering' away underneath. There was less work available for tap dancers, resulting in many changing to other careers; but some ex-stars of vaudeville and films worked in theatres, in nightclubs and on cruise ships. Television work was available, but suited only those artists who were able to create a new act for each show: the practice of repeating the same act throughout a year had been fine for touring theatres, but it was not a viable option for television.

Nevertheless, tap continued to be taught all over the world. Although not as popular as when 'Shirley Temple' was blazoned on the cinema marquees, the studios were still providing tap classes, and many of the ex-show business dancers transferred to the teaching profession.

RENAISSANCE

In the 1970s there was renewed interest in tap. The revival of the musical shows such as *No, No, Nannette* and *42nd Street* paved the way for the resurgence of tap. In the 1970s Broadway was the home of several successful productions featuring tap dance. In the movie industry, films such as *The Boyfriend*, *Steppin' Out*, *Tap* and *The Cotton Club* pioneered a new lease of life for tap in the cinema.

Carol Ball who was 'Any Time Annie' in the West End production of 42nd Street.

Twiggy learned to tap dance especially for the film *The Boyfriend* in the early 1970s. Gillian Gregory, who was also the choreographer for the film, had the pleasure of teaching her at the dance centre in Floral Street. She also taught Amy McDonald when she was about to appear in the 1969/70 production of *Lady Be Good*. On Broadway, Gillian won a Tony Award for her choreography in *Me and My Gal*.

The West End production of *42nd Street* ran for four and a half years, from 1984, providing opportunities for many tap dancers. Carol Ball, already a West End star, played *Any Time Annie* for the complete run. In a chequered career covering theatre, television and films, Carol appeared in the film of *The Boyfriend*, on television in the Benny Hill Show, and in the West End in *Hello Dolly* (when she understudied Carol Channing). Her favourite production was *Mack and Mabel* when she played 'Lottie' and danced *Tap Your Troubles Away*.

Graeme Henderson played Billy Lawlor in *42nd Street*. He learned to tap from three years old, and his early influence was American tap taught to him by his mother. *A Drop of Fred* – a story based on tap dancing – was the theme of an act he performed at Edinburgh Festival in 1992. Then, with a wealth of experience in theatre, he commenced on a project called Ghtap, encouraging talented young dancers and bringing tap back into the mainstream of theatre and the media.

Catherine Zeta Jones played opposite Graeme in *42nd Street*, in the leading role of Peggy Sawyer.

On British television in *The Hot Shoe Show*, Wayne Sleep provided new inspiration for tap. The series included clever choreography from Bill Drysdale, whose expertise has involved him in theatre, teaching and writing. After a West End debut in *Hello Dolly*, starring Mary Martin, he had an extensive career in musicals, television and films.

Gregory Hines

One of the most important stars in the revival of tap is Gregory Hines who, with his appearance on the big screen, provided a new inspiration for the dance world. As a child he had danced with his brother Maurice, and he had admired and been influenced by many of the great tappers, such as Fayard and Harold Nicholas, Bunny Briggs, Gene Kelly, Gene Nelson, and his own teacher, Henry Le Tang. In the late 1970s and the 1980s his numerous film successes included *The Cotton Club*, and starring with Mikhail Baryshnikov in *White Nights*. In his television sitcom, *The Gregory Hines Show*, which started in 1997, his intricate rhythms and expressive performances were equally entertaining in group and solo dances. The incredible accuracy of his interpretation of Bill 'Bojangles' Robinson's staircase dance was proven in the culmination of the film *The Cotton Club*, when the footage of both dancers was blended together at the end of the film.

THE NEXT GENERATION INNOVATORS

Another group of expert tappers had different ideas – and some would take tap away from the musical and vaudeville image. In vaudeville, tap dancing was interspersed with songs and jokes in a mixed variety bill; in musical shows and films, routines had been blended into a story-line – usually light romance.

A complete evening's entertainment of tap dance had not been considered viable (Paul Draper was one of the few dancers who had previously attempted such a programme). When three dancers and three musicians suggested creating such a concert, the veterans met the idea with reservations: they could not imagine an audience sitting through a whole evening of tap dancing. However, in 1979 Jazz Tap Ensemble (based in Los Angeles) was formed

and, with its complete repertoire of tap dance, was an immediate success.

Jazz Tap Ensemble

The company toured concert halls in the USA, in Europe, in England and in South Asia; there was no scenery, the lighting was minimal, and they wore ordinary clothes. The emphasis was on the artistic quality of the performance. The variation in tone, the security of the rhythm, and the clarity of the beating to blend with the playing of the musicians, were of paramount importance. Low-heeled tap shoes are the ideal footwear for achieving such excellence, but such shoes can look unattractive when worn with a dress: the trousers worn by the female members provided the right appearance. The co-founders were Lynn Dally, Fred Strickler and Camden Richmond.

Lynn Dally, the artistic director, is tireless in her work for the world of tap dance, and has given

Sam Weber and Mark Mendonca of Jazz Tap Ensemble. (Jazz Tap Ensemble)

ABOVE: **Lynn Dally, artistic director of Jazz Tap Ensemble. (Jazz Tap Ensemble)**

ABOVE RIGHT: **Linda Sohl-Donnel and Eddie Brown with Jardine Wilson in the background. (Philip Canning, courtesy of Rhapsody in Taps)**

RIGHT: **Eddie Brown with Althea Waites at the piano (1991). (Rhapsody in Taps)**

many dancers the opportunity to dance with the company, particularly the younger generation. Her father, who stressed the importance of musicality, taught Lynn, and in her youth she watched many renowned hoofers.

More Tap Companies

In 1981 'Rhapsody in Taps' was founded. The company is based in Los Angeles and tours concert arenas with a repertoire of diverse works. The modern dance background of artistic director Linda Sohl-Donnel is evident in many of the choreographed arrangements. Sam Weber and Fred Strickler are also contributors to the works of the company. Eddie Brown performed regularly with the company.

Eddie Brown's fast rhythm tap was achieved with minimal, almost imperceptible, movement of the foot. His clever rhythms and dexterity of footwork, together with his patient, friendly nature, made him a popular teacher during his years in Los Angeles. In his early dance career he was part of the exciting development of tap. He had been a member of Bill 'Bojangles' Robinson's company, and for many years shadowed 'Mr Robinson' in his famous dance 'Doin' The New Low Down'. Later in his career he danced with Rhapsody in Taps.

The American Tap Orchestra, founded in 1986, is based in New York. Brenda Bufalino (director and choreographer) first performed in the latter years of

Fred Strickler, dancer, choreographer and teacher. (Lois Greenfield)

vaudeville. Later she studied with Stanley Brown, learning the art of presenting tap as part of an orchestra to jazz and bepop music. The company developed this art with an original approach of a 'concert orchestra of taps'.

Fred Strickler

Tap continues to develop and expand, and Fred Strickler, directing his own company, 'New Ideas on Tap', is innovative in his choreography. Playing around with steps and rhythms he invents some interesting and unusual variations in combinations, and is particularly adept at manipulating rhythms for classical music. Many of his performances have been with symphony and philharmonic orchestras, including the National Symphony for an audience of 70,000 on the National Mall in Washington, D.C. In his frequent solo performances he includes his choreographic version of Morton Gould's 'Tap Dance Concerto', as well as a solo entitled 'Tacit Understanding' to great acclaim. A professor of the University of California, Riverside, his master classes and workshops have taken him to many parts of the world.

Sam Weber

Sam Weber is a member of Jazz Tap Ensemble, but he also choreographs for Rhapsody in Taps, and he has developed his own unique technique. Based originally on the work he did with his teacher Stanley Kahn and that of Jimmy Slyde, he employs clever use of the leg, which leaves the foot completely relaxed and free, enabling him to execute a phenomenal number of sounds within one leg movement. His master classes provide new and exciting challenges. He has appeared with many of the veterans of tap, as well as on television, and he appeared in the German film *Zwei Im Frack*, which premièred in 2001. His repertoire includes many well known pieces, and he is one of the few dancers performing his own choreography of 'Tap Concerto'.

Jimmy Slyde

A veteran and a dancer with extraordinary artistic skills, Jimmy Slyde has great depth of musicality and imagination, and is considered one of the greatest rhythmical tap dancers who influenced many (including Sam Weber). He was born James Godbolt, the change of name occurring because of the remarkable sliding action he and his partner incorporated in their tap choreography (the slide has since become popular). His sensitivity and his attention to tone and melody are a hallmark of his teaching.

ABOVE: Sam Weber, choreographer, dancer and teacher. (Courtesy of Sam Weber)

Jim Taylor was one of the last partners of the legendary Ginger Rogers and toured the world with her for four years in her last nightclub act. They are seen here, dancing together, as well as on the portraits inset. (Main photograph and inset portraits by Oscar Abolafia)

Stanley Kahn

Kahn was a clever teacher who also devised a 'shorthand' method for notating steps; he called it 'Kahnotation'. Each symbol describes a foot action and sound, and when learned, proves a speedy method for recording steps. Sam Weber makes extensive use of this valuable system, and copies are available for general use.

Jim Taylor

Due to an injury sustained whilst choreographing for the fiftieth anniversary production of *The Wizard of Oz*, Jim Taylor has discovered the benefits of the Feldenkraise Method. It is a re-educating process of the central nervous system that increases range of motion, and he has adapted the method successfully for the teaching of tap. He learned tap through working out with such people as Eleanor Powell, Steve Condos and Hermes Pan, during which time he developed a variety of styles. His main focus is to blend 'rhythm' and 'show' tap, and in teaching sessions he encourages students to present and project their work. In a career on stage, in television and in movies he featured with Ginger Rogers, Debbie Reynolds and Julie Andrews, and has danced and choreographed in Hollywood, New York and London.

Amongst other things he is the official tap teacher for the Bob Fosse Foundation.

Special Music Composition for Tap

An interesting musical arrangement composed by **Morton Gould**, Tap Dance Concerto, includes a part that specifically defines the rhythm expected of the tap dancer. The original choreographer was **Danny Daniels**, who performed the concerto in December 1952, with the composer conducting the Rochester Pops Orchestra at the Eastman Theatre in Rochester, New York. Since that date there have been others who have choreographed the concerto, notably Fred Strickler, Sam Webber and Lane Alexander. An unusual performance with the Long Beach Symphony Orchestra in 1997 featured all three dancers, each performing their own arrangement simultaneously.

National Tap Day

On 7 February 1989 a resolution was made declaring 25 May 1989 (the 111th birthday of Bill 'Bojangles' Robinson) as National Tap Dance Day. Organizations throughout America were encouraged to hold celebrations on 25 May each year to honour and practise the art of tap dancing, and to bring it into the public spotlight.

Itinerant Dancing Masters

The age-old 'itinerant dancing master' still exists. Nowadays their travels take them further afield, spanning countries and continents rather than villages. Germany, Belgium, Finland, Japan and many other countries host tap classes.

Interestingly, Steve Condos, amongst his extensive travels, visited France where his brothers had danced in earlier days. He is one of the theatricals who died 'in harness': at a performance in the south of France he left the stage and, with the applause still ringing in his ears, breathed his last.

In the 1980s **Joy Hewitt** spent six years in the south of France, teaching for Rosella Hightowers in Cannes and arranging master classes with visiting tap teachers from America and Britain. Her generosity of spirit and constant desire to share a much-loved subject meant that she was always introducing tappers to each other, and this resulted in the forging of many new friendships. A clever and rhythmic dancer, she spent much of her career teaching and choreographing in Hollywood. During her years in France she inspired a new community of tap dancers, and on her return to the USA she continued to teach with just as much verve and energy.

TAP FESTIVALS AND HOLIDAY CAMPS

Colorado, California, Texas and Washington D.C. are some of the venues hosting holiday courses, tap festivals and summer camps. Many of the experts who travel the world gather at these functions, providing exciting opportunities to learn with new experts as well as old.

Many of the old masters were unrecognized in their own time, and the renaissance gave veterans of the golden age of tap a welcome opportunity to share their talent and experience. In the latter part of their lives people such as Honi Cole, Steve Condos, Eddie Brown, Harold Nicholas, Buster Brown and many others, imparted their specialist knowledge; and it is still possible to see the likes of Fayard Nicholas, Leonard Reed, Jimmy Slyde, Cholly Atkins, Brenda Bufalino and many of their contemporaries. Fayard continues to give sound advice to youngsters, emphasizing the importance of classical lessons to strengthen movement and to create sensitive hand movements (he uses his own hands artistically to demonstrate his point).

Leonard Reed entertains his audience with amusing stories of his days in show business, and continues to monitor performances of the Shim Sham Shimmy; thus the new generation of masters provides a positive link with the young enthusiasts. Experts such as Sam Weber, Fred Strickler, Linda Sohl-Donnel, Lynn Dally, Jim Taylor, Barbara Duffy, Dianne Walker, following in the footsteps of the itinerant dancing masters of another century, also travel in many parts of the world sharing their knowledge.

Jimmy Slyde, skilled veteran and master.

James 'Buster' Brown, a veteran tap dancer who was one of the élite group of masters, and member of the Copasetic Club.

One of the highlights at the culmination of many festivals is to watch these new masters performing 'The Hoofers' Circle' alongside the veterans.

MASTER CLASSES AND PERFORMANCES IN LONDON

Riverside Studios in Hammersmith and the theatres on the South Bank in London are often host to tap-dancing performances. In the 1980s, Riverside hosted Jazz Tap Ensemble in one of their early performances, when it was also recorded by Channel 4 Television. During their stay there were several Master Classes. Many years later at the same studio Honi Cole, gave a fascinating talk on the history of tap, supported by illuminating descriptions and demonstrations of the styles of the various innovators.

His performance of his own creations was equally entertaining. Also appearing on the programme were Chuck Green, a protégé of John Bubbles, and Will Gaines, who was described as 'a living exponent of the Bebop era'.

Bebop Tapper

Will Gaines learned his art by watching the great masters, particularly Teddy Hale; but his rhythmic expertise emanated from listening to jazz musicians. As a schoolboy he spent time tapping, drumming and jamming with other musicians, and by the late 1940s he became a professional dancer, eventually sharing the arena with such 'greats' as Buster Brown, Baby Laurence, Bunny Briggs and Peg Leg Bates. Having performed with Cab Calloway at the famous Cotton Club, he travelled in

America and Canada as well as in Europe, and then settled in London in 1963. He has done much to influence and assist younger dancers in his style of tap. His rhythms are intricate and often delicate, and his improvisational skills are such that he can hold his own with orchestras and jazz groups alike.

His entertaining style is that of the original hoofers, the footwork being the priority, with little or no use of the arms; and his exuberant personality is infectious. He has a unique way of combating the sound problems so often evident in tap-dancing performances: his own small platform of plywood is carried on to the stage and a microphone placed strategically to ensure that his sounds blend with those of the musicians. Thus his rhythm becomes an integral part of the musical soirée.

One of the most interesting and illuminating demonstrations of Will's skills was in 1985 when Sam Sherry (of The Five Sherry Brothers) shared a performance with him at the Shaw Theatre in London; it served to establish a definite link between clog

dancing and tap dancing. Sam, who had made the transition from clogging to tapping at the beginning of the century, reverted to his roots and presented clogging. The similarity of the rhythms and steps performed by these two veterans, each presenting their own original dance form, was irrefutable evidence of the link between the two dance styles.

Revival of the John Tiller Girls

During the 1960s the John Tiller Girls made regular appearances in variety shows as well as on the BBC's *The Billy Cotton Band Shows* and in ATV's *Sunday Night at the London Palladium*. Almost twenty years later, in December 1988, nine of the Tiller Girls appeared in a Christmas show at the Royal Albert Hall. In April 1989, sixteen of the 'Sixties' Tiller Girls were engaged to appear in a 'single performance' at a charity show for Terry Thomas. They have since appeared in approximately 140 charity shows throughout the country, expertly managed by Bruce Vincent with routines set by Wendy Clark

ABOVE: *The 1960s Tiller Girls: 'The Five Past Eight Show' with Max Bygraves at the Alhambra Theatre. (Photograph courtesy of Bruce Vincent)*

LEFT: *Will Gaines, born in America, has spent much of his career dancing in England. (Angela Heskett)*

(a Tiller from 1949–68). Royal occasions included the Queen's 'Forty Glorious Years', the Duke of Edinburgh's eightieth birthday, and the Queen's Golden Jubilee.

Challenges and Record Makers

Throughout the history of tap, challenges and competition and the desire for perfection have been a driving force in its progress. In the 1970s Roy Castle established another kind of challenge.

Records are constantly being made and broken, and Roy Castle was always ready to set a challenge; his enterprising ideas raised thousands of pounds for charity. For example, in 1973 he set the record for the most sounds per second made by a tap dancer, achieving twenty-four per second.

Then in 1977 he and 500 young tappers set the record for the largest tap group. The event was held at the BBC studios in Shepherds Bush. Dressed in an immaculate white suit with black shirt and white tie, he performed a song-and-dance number in the studio, with full orchestra. Then, after a 'slide' in the style of Jimmy Slyde, he danced into the central open-air circle of the BBC's famous circular studio complex. The 500 young tap dancers were set in a circle reminiscent of Busby Berkley, and the performance culminated with Roy dancing under the fountain.

Eleven years later, Roy was on 34th Street, New York, when Macy's Store took up the challenge. There were 4,497 tap dancers. However, an entry in the 2002 publication of the *Guinness Book of Records* credits Macy's with beating this record by producing 6,776 tappers performing a two-minute routine on 34th Street on 17 August 1997.

Another tap-dance record was established in 1997: apparently the greatest distance ever danced was in Red Bank, New Jersey on 31 August. The routine lasted seven hours and crossed several railway tracks, covering a distance of 45.44km (28.24 miles). Roy's 1985 challenge on BBC beat the number of hours set by the New Jersey group – he danced for 23 hours 44 minutes – but with an added interest: he set out to make 1,000,000 sounds within the 24 hours, and reached his target with 16 minutes to spare.

Ever ready to tap his feet, there was an occasion when, having been invited to present the prizes at the Star Tap Awards, to the delight of everyone present he took his shoes out of his pocket, put them on, and proceeded to dance.

The Star Tap Awards

For any aspiring tap dancer, the annual Star Tap Awards are inspirational, whether watching or taking part. The awards ceremony was launched in 1977 as an annual event for young dancers. Devised in memory of Marjorie Davies, the trophies are presented in her name and that of Victor Leopold; there is also a prize for response in class work donated by Moyra Gay, whose rhythmically clever sequences are part of the syllabus for medal examinations. In the years since its inauguration, the level of performance

Roy Castle dancing with a group of 'All Star Record Breakers'. (Reproduced with permission from the BBC)

FAR LEFT: Marjorie Davies of Bush Davies Schools. (Courtesy of Joyce Percy and Daphne Peterson)

LEFT: Victor Leopold of Bush Davies Schools. (Courtesy of Paul Kimm)

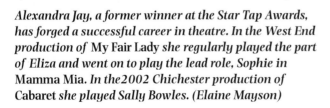

Alexandra Jay, a former winner at the Star Tap Awards, has forged a successful career in theatre. In the West End production of My Fair Lady *she regularly played the part of Eliza and went on to play the lead role, Sophie in* Mamma Mia. *In the 2002 Chichester production of* Cabaret *she played Sally Bowles. (Elaine Mayson)*

Douglas Mills, a former winner at the Star Tap Awards, joined the cast of Tap Dogs. *He has since adjudicated at the awards, and the photograph shows him giving a tap class at an imperial congress. (Elaine Mayson)*

of the candidates has grown in excellence. The rippling tap technique reflects the strength of the syllabus, which is the basis of their training. Many former winners and contestants have forged careers in theatre or in teaching and examining, and some have returned to join the adjudicating panel for the next generation.

SOUTH BANK SHOWS

In 2002 London's South Bank hosted two most interesting productions containing tap. *New York On Tap* featured dancers from America and Britain, and amongst those performing were Brenda Duffy and Marshall Davis (USA), Will Gaines and the Clark Brothers. Jimmy and Steve Clark, two Americans who settled in England, provided audiences with a rare opportunity to see a stylish and polished act from the golden era of tap. They had worked in New York, Chicago, Las Vegas and Hollywood, and in 1948 accepted an offer to work in England, which eventually became their home country.

In the same season *Follies – The Legendary Musical* was staged at the Royal Festival Hall. This exquisite production told the story (through a reunion of the characters) of the glamorous days of the Ziegfeld Follies. The talented choreographer, David Needham – a clever and exacting taskmaster whose choreography included a rhythmical tap number – produced perfection through meticulous attention to detail. His original dance training was tap, although his career has encompassed musical theatre, modern dance, being principal dancer with the Northern Ballet Theatre, and producing award-winning choreographies for many musical shows.

PRESENT TAP HEROES

A New Star
Tap dancing has now entered a new era, and the new young tap hero is Savion Glover, who is considered the best tap dancer ever. His astonishing fast rhythm tap is unchallenged and unbeatable. At a very young age he became a star of stage and screen, winning four Tony Awards for his Broadway performance in *Bring in Da' Noise. Bring in Da' Funk*. His confident and professional performance at the

millennium celebrations at the White House displayed rhythmic versatility, and his caring and sensitive introduction of the artists to Mr and Mrs Clinton and their guests showed maturity and experience. He has already formed a company of young dancers following his style.

Australian Success
The Australians have a reputation for a high standard in many styles of dance, and tap is one of them. In the early nineties the staging of tap dance took a monumental leap forward when a young Australian, Dein Perry, choreographed a brand-new show called *Tap Dogs*. As his inspiration he used the sounds of the workplace of the (Australian) Newcastle Steel Works, where he had completed an apprenticeship to become a fitter and turner. While simulating the industrial environment, the rhythms and counter-rhythms of the steps mimicked the sounds of the steel works, the all-male cast dancing on elevated platforms. Costumes of singlets, shorts and flannel shirts were the simple attire, and Blundstone steel-capped workboots with specially developed steel taps replaced the normal tap shoe.

The style of the work was diverse, with some light, rhythmical sequences contrasted with very loud, hard, mechanical-sounding phrases. The use of leg and ankle action was an important feature in obtaining the required level of tone. Arm lines were free, and complemented the body movements. (Dein's earlier choreography for *The Hot Shoe Shuffle* had been more reminiscent of American vaudeville.) He received rave reviews in London's West End, and the show earned him his second 'Olivier' award. After *Tap Dogs* Dein commenced work on another steel show, entitled *Steel City*.

From Britain to New York
Almost a hundred years after Willie Covan had listened to the streetcars, another young man, Warren Carlyle, learned to love the rhythm of the city of New York. As an active child in Norfolk in the 1970s, horse riding, karate and swimming failed to attract him. However, seeing the film *Top Hat* and the inspirational dancing of Fred Astaire sparked a life-long love of tap dancing and rhythm. He heeded advice to learn classical and modern alongside tap, was twice

winner at the Star Tap Awards, and was one of the students training at Bush Davies in its final days. During his training, Gwen Carter was one of the many clever teachers he met. She taught him to slow down and listen, and also to experiment with phrasing. His exciting career took him to the West End and Broadway, he helped to mount the London Production of *Fosse*, appeared in the film *Centre Stage*, and staged *Oklahoma* and *The Producers* on Broadway. From the little boy who could not keep his feet still, to successful choreographer in New York, tap dancing was the catalyst for the rhythm and pace of his life.

Degree In Dance

Robert Reed was responsible for devising the criteria for an Honorary Degree awarded to nine recipients by

Robert Reed, founder, producer and artistic director of the St Louis Tap Festival. (Courtesy of Robert Reed)

At the gala celebration of the Honorary Awards for Tap Dancing. The recipients, from left to right: Cholly Atkins, Henry LeTang, Bunny Briggs, Fayard Nicholas, James 'Buster' Brown, Leonard Reed, James Godbolt a.k. Jimmy Slyde, Jeni LeGon and Prince Spencer. (Courtesy of Robert Reed)

Oklahoma City University. Founder, artistic director and producer of the St Louis Tap Festival, Robert's varied career has involved dancing and choreographing in shows with Sammy Davis Jr, Liberace and Cher, amongst others. He has also toured with Cab Calloway, and conducts workshops in the USA, Brazil, Germany and Finland.

A FITTING TRIBUTE

On 22 February 2002, Oklahoma City University was 'proud to confer honorary Doctor of Performing Arts In American Dance degrees' upon nine tap dancers. It was a well earned tribute to dedicated dancers after long and successful careers. The recipients were **Cholly Atkins**, who danced and choreographed acts for the renowned Cotton Club boys; **Bunny Briggs**, who began dancing in the streets of Harlem in the seventies, and appeared in a documentary *No Maps on My Taps*; **James 'Buster' Brown**, who had a career that spanned seven decades, from touring in vaudeville to performing on Broadway; **James T. Gobolt (Jimmy Slyde)**, a musical tapper who popularized the slide; **Jeni LeGon**, following a successful career in films and the theatre, who continues imparting her knowledge and sharing her talent; **Henry LeTang**, an innovative choreographer and clever teacher; **Fayard Nicholas**, who after a remarkable career still shares his valuable knowledge with young dancers; **Leonard Reed** who, when in his nineties, created a new chorus for the 'Shim Sham Shimmy', calling it 'The Revenge'; **Prince Spencer**, a brilliant rhythm dancer, who was one of the four 'Step Brothers'; these brothers were the first black dancers to appear at Radio City Music Hall. The programme for the Gala celebration and presentation, quoting Martha Graham, declared:

> Great dancers are not great because of their technique; they are great because of their passion.

In a new era of tap dancing, the expertise has reached new heights. The emphasis changes as the stars of the moment influence the style. Ideas are traded or stolen, and the steps and rhythms are modified, developed and improved upon – but the essential elements of the early roots remain.

3 FLOORS, SHOES AND COSTUMES

FLOORS

The floor can be your best friend or your worst enemy, because the quality of the sound produced is of paramount importance. The floor, together with the taps on the shoes, can make or mar a performance. For all forms of dance a slip-resistant, sprung floor, with an even surface is an essential part of the equipment. However, because of the taps on the shoes, the slip factor is a greater hazard for tap dancing than for other styles of dance. The one thing to avoid is a cement floor, as dancing on such a hard surface for any length of time would cause at least backache and at worst more permanent physical damage.

Studios

If planning to hire a hall or studio, it is wise to test the floor before making a commitment; simply dancing on the floor can be very enlightening. If it is concrete, the lack of resilience will be obvious. If the plan is to lay a floor in a newly acquired studio it is advisable to discuss the requirements with a dance floor expert, as a suitable floor can be installed on top of concrete. For tap the best surface for producing clean sound was always maple – although nowadays there are many modern fabrications available. Maple is the most durable wood, and is not easily damaged – an important attribute for withstanding the beating of the metal taps. Oak is also a good surface (although not as strong as maple) but many other types of wood splinter easily. It is advisable to use a sealant both for protection and to remove any slippery element. (Advice is available in Mark Foley's book *Dance Floors*, a detailed survey published by Dance UK.) There are many firms dealing with dance floors, and the Internet has widened accessibility to companies who offer these services.

Roll-Out Floors

Roll-out coverings are available for floors with unsuitable, uneven surfaces. They can be laid permanently or temporarily. Thick floor coverings reproduce a dull tap tone, so it is wiser to opt for the thin variety, which produces clearer, more resonant tones. A range of colours is available to suit individual taste.

Floors in Performance

Many theatres, both small and large, are dancer friendly. Nevertheless, when producing a show or recital the stage should be thoroughly checked for pitfalls, as joins in the flooring, trap doors, culverts and suchlike might cause a dancer to trip unexpectedly. Locate these before a performance, and plan to avoid them whenever possible.

Floors for Rehearsals

Practising at home can be a problem, since very often the best-sounding floor is also the one most treasured by the family. For instance, a beautifully tiled kitchen or a French-polished lounge floor make ideal sounding boards – but scratched surfaces from enthusiastic tappers can very easily infuriate otherwise doting parents. There used to be an answer to that problem in the shape of a portable 'roll-up' tap mat: this was made of narrow strips of maple joined together with hessian or canvas strips, the result a tap mat with good sound, ample protection for precious floors, and a portable piece of equipment. Many a tap dance has been performed at a garden party on such a mat. Bruce Forsyth's description of the ever-increasing size of the one his father made for him is testimony to the support given by parents to their offspring.

Harlequin Flooring has produced an up-to-date answer to this problem in easily portable tap-dance tiles, 36in square, any number of which can be laid safely side by side to provide the required floor size.

Pedestal and Staircase Dancing

There are many stories about incidents concerning floors or dance surfaces, and there are many potential hazards, though most of these can be overcome with foresight and rehearsal. 'Pedestal' dancing was a novelty act for clog dancers, and later for tap dancers in the vaudeville and music hall era; the balance, control, and the precision of footwork required would have necessitated hours of rehearsal. Paul Draper in fact abandoned his attempts to include such an item in his act. Fred Egan was a pedestal dancer in the music halls in the late nineteenth and early twentieth centuries, and his motto ''e can sing, 'e can dance, 'e can do almost anything, Egan' is fondly remembered by his famous granddaughter, Doreen Wells.

Imagine, too, the control necessary for performing the staircase dance of Bill 'Bojangles' Robinson, or the rehearsals required to negotiate the long flights of stairs in *Stormy Weather*, performed with such ease by the Nicholas brothers. But some of today's theatrical productions still require such expertise, and dancers rise to the occasion.

Fred Egan, a pedestal dancer at the turn of the last century. (Harry Drewett)

SHOES

The most important piece of equipment for a tap dancer is a suitable pair of shoes. Glamorous or practical, that is the question for the female of the species (men are luckier, because for them the practical is also the smartest). However, the choice is personal, and the dichotomy provides the ladies with an excuse to add extra pairs of shoes to the wardrobe.

Dealing first with practicalities, proficiency dictates – no, *demands* – that the shoe is comfortable, snug and well fitting. (Socks or tights are essential, as unabsorbed perspiration is bad for the shoes as well as the feet.) The uppers should have a degree of flexibility, since a stiff upper inhibits the movement and therefore reduces the ability to control the footwork. Ideally the sole should be firm and the shoe should be of a reasonable weight. Shoes are made in varying qualities of leather, and the available budget will often be the deciding factor in the final choice.

For a greater degree of expertise the laced-up flat, wide-heeled shoes are the best. They are, of course, less flattering, but are much more controllable,

especially when dancing close rhythm work. A cuban heel can be a good compromise for those who prefer a higher heel, although they should be chosen with care; in some designs, for instance, the heel is cut too steeply. Check the shoe by putting it on a shelf at eye level: ensure that the heel is set properly underneath the back of the shoe, and that the front of the shoe sits flat.

There are occasions when a high-heeled shoe is the only wise choice to blend with a glamorous costume or particular style of dance. Adequate rehearsal should be undertaken to ensure that the dancer is able to cope with the shoes within the choreography of the piece. Ann Miller was remarkable in expertly producing brilliant rhythms in high-heeled tap shoes.

Instep tie is usually cuban heel for an adult shoe, and flat for a child. Its use depends on individual taste.

There are other types of shoe available. Jazz shoes with a very flexible sole and taps attached are lightweight, and a comfortable option for long hours of teaching. However, the sound produced is less adequate than that of the conventional shoe.

A selection of styles in tap shoes.

The weight of the shoe makes an enormous difference to the amount of energy required. Thus to make heavy sounds in a lightweight shoe such as a jazz shoe requires greater tension in the muscles and a more positive foot action, and this often produces a 'dull' sound rather than a 'ringing' tone. A shoe that is at least the weight of a walking shoe requires little or no effort to achieve clear, resonant tones of both heavy and light quality. Whatever the shoe, the footwork should always be sensitive.

As for colour, black, white and beige are widely available, as are two-toned black and white. Shoes can also be dyed to match a chosen outfit.

Taps

Taps for both toe and heel should, where possible, be the same width as the shoe. If an exact fit is not available, a slightly narrower tap is necessary because a tap which protrudes beyond the width of the shoe is dangerous. Metal taps vary in quality; Capezio Teletone taps are amongst the most superior for producing quality in tone. Some shoes are sold with the taps already in place.

Various methods are used to attach taps to shoes: some are fixed with rivets; others (such as Teletone, which have an excellent tone) have a lining next to the shoe, and the tap is screwed to the lining. Some have three screws, and others are secured with one screw in the centre of the tap. The taps should be firmly (but not absolutely tightly) screwed to the shoes so that there is no chance of them rattling. Loose taps mar the clarity of tone; very tight taps might be too dull. The connoisseur would test for the ideal sounds, and would also ensure that toe and heel tap have a matching sound. A screwdriver is an important item of equipment. Loose screws can damage a floor as well as spoil a performance, and all tap dancers should carry a screwdriver and some spare screws for emergencies. Tap-dance repair kits (and velvet shoe bags) are available from Hollywood Tap Mall.

'Soft-shoe' dances were originally performed in a leather walking shoe. The taps were added at a later date.

Wooden-Soled Shoes

Bill Robinson wore wooden-soled shoes. Unlike clogs, which had a sole made out of one complete piece of wood, these shoes had a split sole, in that the wooden sole and heel were fitted on the front and back of the shoe, and the space under the instep was leather, allowing flexibility of movement in the foot.

Experimenting with Sound

Various methods have been tried to enhance the sounds in stepping and tapping. At one stage coins

43

ABOVE: *Dancing clogs. The Cliffe Castle Museum, Keighley, Yorkshire owns this interesting pair of dancing clogs from the late 1800s, early 1900s. Made by a clogger called Martin Welsh of Maryport in Cumbria, they have a jingle screwed into the bottom to enhance the sound. (Ian Ward)*

ABOVE RIGHT: *A pair of modern dancing clogs and a pair of Irish 'step-dancing' shoes. The clogs lace up, and have a thick rim of leather on the bottom. The Irish shoes lace up with a strap across the ankle. The fibre glass on the toes and heels makes a distinctive sound, quite different from metal taps.*

ABOVE: *Doreen Wells. (Anthony Crickmay)*

LEFT: *A selection of attractive tap shoes belonging to Doreen Wells. (Harry Drewett)*

were fixed to the bottom of clogs; the Irish hammered nails into the soles of their shoes; African dancers put bottle caps between their toes. After the plain metal taps were introduced for tap dancing there were many experiments with various types, including taps with a jingle sound (the tap was made in two parts, a separate piece of metal being screwed to the centre of the tap to make a rattling sound). However, much better rhythms are produced from the single piece of metal.

Shoes for Theatre and in Films

The shoes worn by the chorus girls in the Cotton Club were instep tie with large bows on the front, but the soubrette or solo dancer also did 'toe dancing' with taps fitted on the tips of pointe shoes.

Dancers such as Ann Miller, Ginger Rogers, Eleanor Powell, Jeni LeGon and Ruby Keeler all looked attractive and feminine, and their shoes were chosen carefully to complement their costumes. Doreen Wells was of the opinion that the shoe should be an elegant extension of the leg, rather than a clumsy appendage.

Shoes should be chosen to fit the occasion, both in colour and style. Alternatively, for those occasions when security of footwork for rhythm or close work requires a flat, mundane shoe, designing an outfit to match can solve the problem; it can still be attractive. If an elegant costume design is the primary concern, then ideally the shoes should be complementary. For class work the shoe should be comfortable and well fitting.

Male Dancers
Men's tap shoes are available in varying qualities. The most usual style is the Oxford lace-up shoe in black, white, beige or two tones (usually black and white). There is also a high top, pull-on tap shoe called a 'Wellington' that was used in the Broadway show *Walking Happy*, an ankle-height boot with an elastic insert on both the inside and the outside, made in various colours of suede and leather. There is also the Oxford shoe that Fred Astaire used to wear, called a 'Spectator', a white tap shoe with black toe-pieces and heel cover, and a black insert where the shoe-strings lace. These are now custom-made in every imaginable colour, including silver metallic.

COSTUMES AND PRACTICE CLOTHES

Clothes for class work should be comfortable and well fitting, but should allow ease of movement with no undue restrictions. Anything loose that could trip people over, should be avoided. Many teachers stipulate a standard uniform requirement for their school, and these rules should be strictly observed.

Dancewear companies sell very attractive outfits suitable for both studio wear and theatre; these encompass an infinite variety of styles in leotards and tights, trousers, crop-tops, tracksuits and T-shirts. The comfortable range of fabrics includes velvet, lycra and cotton, and there is something to suit every fad in design.

For performances, the theatre costume catalogues are full of attractive, ready-made designs, to suit almost any type of choreography.

Shoe styles have changed very little during the history of tap dance. Costumes have gone through a series of dramatic fashion changes and developments, as well as retaining (or returning to) some of the popular styles of earlier days. Evening dress complete with top hat was the most popular wearing apparel for male dancers, as well as business suits with waistcoats (with or without a bowler hat). Leonard Reed and Willie Bryant changed outfits for each of their three daily performances: they wore dapper suits in the afternoon, tailored suits for the dinner performance, and in the evening they changed into top hat, white tie and tails.

There was, and still is, a multitude of character costumes, such as clown, military and sailor outfits. Casual and very casual clothes also became popular, although the smart suit is still favoured by many. For the ladies, the outfits ranged from a variety of glamorous dresses and 'showgirl' leotards, to shorts with puffed-sleeve blouses and many designs of trouser suit. Many of these styles have survived, but the modern costume wardrobe also includes business suits for women as well as some very attractive catsuits with bell-bottoms, and many more attractively designed trousers and tops.

Nowadays most children's outfits are more sophisticated. Boys are sometimes less formal, but often wear smart trousers, shirts and possibly braces.

Some children from the 1940s and 1950s in costume.
(centre: Ivor E. Lewis; left and right: photographer unknown)

Young dancers from 2001 (winners at the Star
Tap Awards). (Photographs by Elaine Mayson)

4 MUSIC AND RHYTHM, TECHNIQUE AND CHOREOGRAPHY

MUSIC

Music is the inspiration for dancing, whatever the form of dance. Whether listening to ragtime, swing-time, jazz, blues, boogie, rock or bebop (classical still being a favourite of some), a tap dancer will want to rattle the feet.

Jazz music is a combination of complex African rhythms and European harmonic structure, and developed during the same period as tap dancing. Brass bands were touring at the same time as minstrel shows in the latter part of the nineteenth century. Ragtime developed in the 1890s. This syncopated music with its structure based on the march was popularized by the compositions of Scott Joplin. Gradually, as jazz music evolved, it acquired a flowing rhythmic quality that was smoother than the rag. Various developments such as swing, boogie woogie (with its walking bass), blues (adaptations from the songs of plantation workers and the hymns they sung in church) and rock were all inspirational accompaniments for tap dancers.

Bebop arrived in the 1940s. It was faster and less suitable for dance, but it eventually inspired many tappers, particularly the dancers whose forte was improvisation. Add to these the Latin rhythms, the various waltzes and the compositions with unusual time signatures, and there is a never-ending list of challenging music to interpret.

For tap dancing, a regular beat is necessary, and there should be spaces for rhythmic development. It is wiser to avoid rhythmically full arrangements.

Choosing Music

Some music is 'even', some is 'swing' with a triplet quality, other compositions lend themselves to the use of both even and triplet rhythms. Most music is composed in eight-bar phrases, with or without an extension, some arrangements are twelve bars, and there are also other formats. The basic rhythm of each type gives a starting point for arrangements.

Some Examples
Ragtime (ragged time) – even rhythm.
Boogie, often a twelve-bar phrase – even or triplet rhythm.
Rock – even time. Usually a twelve-bar phrase.
Swing – uses 12th notes and 8th note triplets.
Blues – could be even or triplet timing. Usually a twelve-bar phrase.
Tango – there are many types of tango, most in even time. Two examples follow:

Tango in 2/4 time (even) – the basic rhythm is $\underline{1}$ + ( ) + $\underline{3}$ $\underline{4}$ with a positive emphasis on each count. *(For convenience counting this 2/4 tango, the counts shown represent the four quavers in the bar.)*

Tango in 4/4 time – even – the basic rhythm of $\underline{1}$ $\underline{2}$ $\underline{3}$ $\underline{4}$ + has equal emphasis on each count.

Bosanova and beguine – 1+ ( ) + 3 + 4 + even rhythm, but with a softer quality than a tango, and it is sometimes possible to dance triplets (12th notes) comfortably between the beats.

The musical notation shows two different types of 'tango' rhythm, one in 2/4 time and one in 4/4 time.

Waltz – could be even, or 12th note triplet rhythm.

Careful listening to the chosen music is advisable to see whether even or swing or both could be used.

ANALYSIS OF RHYTHM FOR TEACHING

Demonstration is the most effective method of teaching; the innate rhythmical dancer will automatically hear and interpret the rhythms correctly. However, counting of rhythms will be necessary at some stage. Counts are the tools of the trade and can be recited rhythmically, but mnemonic phrases are also useful. 'Thanks for the Buggy Ride' or 'And Thanks for the Buggy Ride' are often used for buck or pick-up time-steps. Probably the most successful verbal illustrations are phrases such as 'da diddle de dada' or 'parradiddle de' spoken with the relevant rhythmic intonation. However, for accuracy in print, counts are more reliable. First, let us deal with the various elements involved in music and rhythm.

Time

Time is the regular pulse (like a heartbeat). People usually walk 'in time'. The tempo may vary, but the pulse is regular. The time signature at the beginning of a musical score denotes the amount and type of note contained in a bar of music: for example 4/4 = four quarter notes or crotchet beats; 3/4 = three quarter notes or crotchet beats; 2/4 = two quarter notes or crotchet beats. (There are also compound time signatures such as 6/8 and 12/8, but the analysis that follows will deal only with simple time signatures and their development.)

Tempo

The tempo is the speed at which the music is played. The tempo recommendation for the exercises is given as a metronome marking. Metronome markings are often used to denote speed (e.g. 'crotchet (quarter note) = 120' means that there are 120 crotchets per minute). In the sequences the number will refer to the quarter for the dancer.

Rhythm

Rhythm is expressive time. It is a recurring pattern of varying note values, accents and missed beats, within the discipline of time.

Quarter notes represent the regular pulse or timekeepers. Fitting other note values (8th, 12th, and 16th notes) between the pulse beat, constitutes rhythm. Missed beats and syncopation are also elements of rhythm. Being percussive sound, tap does not use half notes and whole notes (except in the occasional movements such as a toe-beat drag or a slide). In fact there is no difference in the length of any of the note values in tap; it is the spaces between that determine the value attributed to each sound.

'Clusters' and 'Grace Notes'

The sounds in some steps, such as four-sound cramp rolls, are grouped tightly together, the four sounds often being achieved within the last 16th of the count. These will be referred to as 'clusters'.

Another element of rhythm is when two sounds are fitted tightly together, the first occurring a split second before the second, and the second exactly on the beat. These are described by musicians as 'grace notes' and by drummers as a 'flam'.

Syncopation

Syncopation is to put an accent in an unusual or unexpected place: it is deliberately to disturb the beat by moving the accent away from the strong beats and on to the weaker ones. The strongest beat of a bar is the first, and, in 4/4 time, the third will be the next in strength. Counts two and four are the weak beats (four being weaker than two). Accenting the off beats (two or four) creates syncopation. Accenting the 8th, 12th or 16th notes between the beat develops syncopation further. In each case the next beat (or part of the beat) is missed or simply weakened.

Syncopation is sometimes described as 'borrowing' or 'stealing' (usually less than a 16th note value) from the previous beat or bar. The musician 'pushes' the first beat of the bar by hitting the note just before the downbeat, and then sustaining it into the count. This element is evident in many of the rags. Listen particularly to the playing of ragtime by Winifred Atwell and James Raeburn on CD.18 and CD.23 (*see* p.124).

Tacit and Missed Beats

Tacit is a period of silence, usually a bar or more. Missed beats are silence for one, or a specific number, of beats. Both are important parts of rhythm. Missed beats and tacit in the dancers' rhythm give highlight to the following and preceding sounds. Tacit, when used by the musician, is an excellent test to check the dancer's ability to sustain the tempo.

Stop-Time

This is the regular occurrence of missed beats in a phrase of music, for example:

1 - 3 - 5 - 7 8 1 - 3 - - 6 7 - 1 - 3 4 - 6 7 8 1 2 - - - 6 7 -

Any combination of missed and 'played' notes can be used, and the choice depends on the melody. The spaces in the music are ideal opportunities for 'busy' tap sequences, rather like a musician's solo in jazz improvisation sessions.

Even Rhythm

Even 8th and 16th notes will be given as: 1+2+3+4+5+6+7+8+ and: 1e+a2e+a3e+a4e+a respectively. Where there is a mixture of even 8th and 16th notes between beats, the relevant 'e' or 'a' will be omitted, *e.g.* 1 +a2 +a3 or 1e+ 2e+ 3e+.

Swing Rhythm

This is 8th note triplets (or accented 8th notes) and 12th notes: 1 a2 a3 a4 and: 1&a2&a3&a4&a.

The musical notation for the counts of quarter notes, even eighth notes and sixteenth notes.

Two different versions of the method of writing the musical notation for the counts of quarter notes, eighth-note triplets (accented eighth notes) and twelfth notes.

Mixing Even and Swing

There are occasions when both types of count have been used within the same sequence: this is deliberate. Some sequences require even 8th notes as well as 12th notes to be evenly spaced between the beats, and some music works well with these mixed-note values. The rhythm might be, for example: 1 +2 +3 +4 &a5&a6 + 7 + 8.

Extra Sounds

For the steps which, like the Maxi-ford, divide the beat into five (20ths), 'n' has been inserted into the counts: 1e+na2 or 1&nna.

Clusters

Clusters, such as the rhythm of a four-sound cramp roll, are noted as 'nna1', and grace notes as 'n1'.

Confusion can arise when the sequence starts before count '1' e.g. '+ 1'. For example, to double even 8th notes to 16th notes, the result would be as follows:

+ 1 + 2 + 3 + 4 + 5 + 6 + 7 + 8
a 1e + a 2e + a 3e + a4 e+

To arrive at 16th notes leading to count '1', i.e. 'e+a1' it is necessary to start with +8 in the original rhythm. The original rhythm is on the top line, and the doubled rhythm underneath:

+ 8 + 1 + 2 + 3 + 4 + 5 + 6 + 7
e + a1 e+a 2e +a3 e+a 4

It each example, the rhythm pattern is completed in one bar, instead of two bars.

The musical notation for quarter notes, grace notes (or flam) and a cluster of sounds.

Missed Beats

Missed beats are in italic and in brackets *(4)*. In some sequences italic brackets have been used to show a missed 8th or 16th note between the beat, e.g. *(a)* or *( )*.

Syncopation

Off-beats that require accent are underscored, e.g. '2' , '&' or 'e' , and so on.

Doubling Up

To double up, simply take a sequence, and then take it at twice the speed but retaining the same accent. The count of '1' must stay in the same place in both versions: thus 1 3 5 7 in the original become 1 2 3 4 in the doubled version, and 2 4 6 8 from the original become the '+' sounds between the counts. The example below gives the counts of the original, and the doubled version underneath.

1 2 3 4 5 6 7 8   1 + 2 + 3 + 4 + 5 + 6 + 7 + 8 +
1 + 2 + 3 + 4 +   1 e + a 2 e + a 3 e + a 4 e + a

It is useful to understand the analysis of these doubled rhythms, but in practice it is much easier to count at twice the speed: it is less cumbersome and obviates the chance of error. The Maxi-ford analysis in the Traditional Steps section is an example of this method.

Cross Phrasing

By creating a phrase of dance that is either longer or shorter than the musical phrase, and then dancing it twice or more without space between, the dancer's phrase will cross the musical phrase. The result makes an interesting and unexpected phrase of rhythm, and by retaining the original accent, also creates syncopation. In 4/4 music the dancer's phrase could, for example, be six, seven, nine or ten counts to achieve the desired result.

In 3/4 time a dancer's phrase of five, seven or eight counts would produce the same effect. The result will be more impressive if the dancer's phrase has a strong start, with a finish that fades away.

AN AID TO LEARNING RHYTHMS

Well-known verses and nursery rhymes are ideal for helping to teach rhythms. Take for example *Humpty Dumpty*. It is perfect for initiation to 8th note triplets and 12th notes. First recite the rhyme and analyse the rhythm, then use simple steps to interpret the rhythm.

Humpty Dumpty sat on a wall
Humpty Dumpty had a great fall
All the king's horses and all the king's men
Couldn't put Humpty together again.

The rhythm is:
1a2 a3&a4 5 a6 a7&a8 1&a2&a3&a4
5&a6&a7&a8

Choose some basic steps to match the rhythm, for example:
Step ball-change shuffle ball change step (twice).
Step (once): Shuffle spring (three times).
Step (once). Pick-up spring step (three times).

To teach even 8th notes try:

Sing a song of sixpence, a pocket full of rye,
Four and twenty blackbirds, baked in a pie.

The rhythm is:
1+2+3 4+5+6+7 (8). 1+2+3 4 5 6+7 (8)

And an example of basic steps is:
Step heel-beat (twice), step (once), step heel-beat (three times), stamp (once), pause. Step heel-beat (twice). Step (three times) step heel-beat (once) toe-beat. Pause.

To practise commencing on the count of '8' use the well-known song, *76 Trombones*.

Seventy six trombones lead the big parade,
With a hundred and ten cornets close at hand
They were followed by rows and rows of the finest
virtuosos, The cream of ev'ry famous band.

and choreograph steps to the relevant counts of:
8&a1 2 3 4 a5 a6 (7) &a8&a1 2 3 4 a5 (6 7)
&a8&a1 2 3 4 a5 a6 a7 8 a1 (2) a3 a4 a5 (6 7)

The Limerick at the front of the book, *Rhythm of a Foot Percussion Artist,* is ideal for time steps. Like W. H. Auden's *Night Mail*, Robert Louis Stevenson's *From A Railway Carriage* or Henry Wadsworth Longfellow's *Hiawatha*, the words are most effective when spoken with a machine-like rhythmic quality. Written in the style of an extended limerick, the rhythm is based on that of double time-steps and double breaks (with shuffles) (Nos. 183 and 184).

Sequence of Steps for Limerick

First verse:
*Two double breaks; two double time-steps;
one double break;
Two double time-steps; one double break; two half
breaks (second half); one double break;*
Second verse:
*Two double time-steps: one double break;
two double time-steps; one double break;*
Third verse:
*Two double time-steps; one double break;
two double time-steps; one double break;
Two double time-steps; two double breaks.*

TECHNIQUE

The final aim? Clear, clean, rhythmical sounds with variation in the level of tone and the use of accent. Achieving these depends on weight distribution, leg and foot action, and relaxation (as well as control) in the knees, feet and ankles.

Weight Distribution
The weight should be held slightly forward and over the balls of the feet (knees relaxed), thus ensuring that the heels do not accidentally drop. In steps, springs, hops and many other steps, the sound should be made with the ball of the foot, and if the heel is allowed to drop, it mars the tone.

Careful control is necessary for weight changes. If momentarily off balance, a foot may hit the ground sooner than desired and before the correct rhythmic moment.

Some steps are easier to accomplish if the weight is strategically placed in preparation and/or in execution. Pull-backs and ripples are just two examples.

Leg and Foot Action

Concentrate first on correct leg and foot action, rather than the quality of the sound. The desired tone and rhythm will follow once these are mastered.

Relaxation

In the knees, relaxation assists rhythmic quality. A dry knee will help to achieve a heavier sound; a fluid knee will soften the tone.

In the ankles, the degree of flexibility is less important than the amount of relaxation. Relaxation is the key: an ankle, although flexible, may be tense, and tension mars rhythm and tone.

As regards the feet, some steps require a leg action with a completely relaxed foot, others require control in the foot, and it is important to recognize which is required. Most steps benefit from sensitivity in the feet. Sometimes when practising, imagine that the floor is made of glass, and modify the knee and foot action to avoid breaking the glass.

STYLE

Tap dancers are a motley group of people emanating, as they do, from various backgrounds. Each performs with an individual style overlaying the movements with other forms of dance, or simply dancing as a rhythm dancer with a casual approach to presentation.

Whether dancing for recreation or for a performance, it is beneficial to develop a 'style'. Ideally it should be relaxed and easy, since overdone style often mars a performance. The sound is the most important factor in tap dancing. The arm lines and body movements should occur as a result of the steps, or be used to assist and to balance the movement. For example, in wings some students find it helpful to lift the arms, in pull-backs to hold them at shoulder level, and in turns to extend them sideways. The ideal is minimal use of arms. If dancing as a rhythm tapper, the arms can be held comfortably in front of the body or relaxed at the sides. For those who wish to use the movements developed in other forms of dance, attention should be paid to achieving balanced lines and breadth of movement, but retaining ease and economy of arm movements. In so doing the

occasional hitting of a strong, impressive line will, because it is unexpected, have much more audience impact.

Inner quality, presentation and projection are all part of a final performance. Expressing a mood is usually inspired by the musical accompaniment.

Watching old films and videos of the masters provides a wealth of inspiration for style and for inventing new rhythms.

CHOREOGRAPHY

When choreographing a dance, the overall picture should be considered. This involves rhythmic content, ground pattern, levels of tone and (where applicable) use of arms and body. Highlight and lowlights, mood, style and atmosphere are other important ingredients. The lowlights or 'throw away' sections are most important because they give greater meaning to the highlights. There is no set way to choreograph. Some people start at the beginning and work methodically through to the end, and others start at the end or in the middle.

The following are a few rules of thumb that might be useful:

* First, choose the music; if planning a choreography without music (a cappella), choose a basic rhythm.
* Consider the age and ability of the performer when choosing music, style, rhythms and steps.
* Listen to the music until it is very familiar.
* Establish the rhythmic content of the piece – whether even or swing, and so on.
* Establish the style, mood and atmosphere it suggests.
* Note the length of the piece, and spread the content to ensure a balanced, 'rounded' piece.
* Use rhythms that complement and blend with the musical arrangement.
* Ensure flow of movement as well as rhythm and always include syncopation in tap routines.
* Find the highlights and lowlights, and use them.
* Use varying levels of energy.
* Use a ground pattern that is balanced (probably asymmetrical rather than symmetrical).
* Avoid overloading – leave some spaces.

* Build to a climax, and hold the final position long enough to fix a 'picture' in the minds of the audience – mentally counting slowly to three is a good idea.
* A good opening and a good finish are essential.
* Finally, check that the arrangement interprets the chosen music.

One valuable piece of advice given by Doris Humphreys is: 'Don't leave the end until the end.'

WHERE TO LEARN AND HOW TO FIND OUT

Tap dance lessons are available for recreation purposes, or in preparation for a career in theatre or teaching.

Dancing Lessons for Children and Adults
Dance schools offering classes for children, teenagers and adults exist in most towns and villages. Some enter children and students for examinations.

Details of teachers in your area can be obtained from telephone directories, yellow pages and advertisements in the local paper. The CDET publishes a list of qualified teachers. Examination societies will, on application, provide a list of teachers in a particular area.

Theatre and Teacher Training for Professional Students
Ability, dedication and stamina are necessary prerequisites for full-time training, and such training is available at universities and colleges. Entry to a theatre and teacher training college is normally by audition. College courses (offering dance or musical theatre courses, or a degree in dance) usually last for three years. However, training in another dance form, such as classical ballet or modern dance, is usually expected. It is unlikely that tap dance would provide a full and active career – although there are exceptions. Singing and acting are also recommended. Your present teacher should be able to advise you regarding suitable colleges. Advertisements for the various colleges appear in dance magazines.

Refresher Courses for Teachers
Once qualified, teachers receive an 'in-house' magazine, providing details of activities and courses available for upgrading qualifications and broadening teaching ability. These opportunities vary between societies. Most offer an annual event and regular regional courses, and (some) arrange residential courses.

Holiday Courses and Summer Camps
There are many holiday courses and weekend courses for all age groups and levels. Most offer a variety of dance forms, with tap as part of the course, but some are for tap only.

Specialist tap courses are popular in America, some organized at international festivals, and others by the tap companies. In Britain also there are weekend and day courses run by specialist tap organizations. Details are available from the companies concerned, or in dance magazines. Regional day courses and residential courses are also organized by the examining bodies – again, details are available from the society concerned.

PART TWO

5 THE VOCABULARY OF STEPS

The names of the steps, apart from those of the traditional steps, vary throughout the tap-dancing world. The many 'invented' names are rich and various. In the following chapter the steps have been grouped together in accordance with their similarity and the number of sounds. Some have alternative names, but in general, the first named (or its abbreviation) in each description is the one used in the sequences.

Regarding the technical aspect, the information given strives to describe a method that will produce good results. However, there are other, equally successful techniques. The one aspect upon which every dancer will agree is the importance of the resultant sound. Clarity, variation in tone, security of rhythm, discipline of timing and tempo – all of these are imperative, no matter what decision is made regarding style, artistry and level of performance.

The notation for the sequences is on three separate lines. The first line gives right or left foot (occasionally an extra line is added for ground pattern). The second line describes the steps used (generally a semi-colon is used to denote a change of foot). The third line gives the counts. To facilitate easy recognition, the method used for counting the exercises differs between 'even' and 'swing' rhythm (*see* analysis in chapter 4). Missed beats, or missed parts of beats, are shown in italic and in brackets, e.g. 1 *(2)* 3 + 4.

THE TERMINOLOGY

The steps analysed are a mixture of light, medium and heavy sounds. However, the tone can be changed or controlled in any of the steps where a different level of sound is desired; the descriptions 'light', 'medium' and 'heavy' are simply a guide.

Abbreviations

apt = apart	pll.bk = pull back
b = behind	prog = progressive
bk = back	pu = pick-up
bkds = backwards	pu.chge = pick-up-change
bll.chge = ball change	R = right
brk = break	RCB = right corner back
bsd = beside	RCF = right corner front
chge = change	rev = reverse
clp = clip	RF = right foot
clsd = closed	RL = right leg
crmp.rl = cramp roll	RS = right side
dbl = double	s = sound
diag = diagonally	sd = side
dr. bk = draw back	sdwys = sideways
fk = fake	sep = separate
flt = flat	sh = shuffle
fr = front	sngl = single
ft = foot	sntch = snatch
fwd = forward	str = straight
hl = heel	sup = supporting
heelbt = heel beat	t/s = time-step
ins = inside	tog = together
L = left	tp = tap
LCB = left corner back	trav = travel or travelling
LCF = left corner front	trng = turning
LF = left foot	trpl = triple
LL = left leg	w (or xfer wgt.) = with weight or with a transfer of weight
LOD = line of dance	
LS = left side	
M/F = Maxi-ford	wgt = weight
n = no weight, or without transferring weight	X = across or cross
	Xb = cross behind
opn = open	Xf = cross in front
outs = outside	xfer = transfer
pdle.brk = paddle break	

ONE SOUND

Taps and Brushes

A single sound in which the ball or heel of the foot hits the ground and is then immediately released. These are usually light sounds.

1   Straight tap (str.tap)

Standing on one leg, the working foot is lifted and the heel held approximately alongside the supporting instep. Strike the toe down and immediately up again. The movement comes from the ankle.

2   Progressive tap (prog.tap)

A series of straight taps executed during a gradual movement of the working leg in any direction. These can be taken forward and away from the supporting foot, sideways across in front of the supporting foot; or commencing with the working foot stretched in front of the supporting foot, and then executing a series of taps back towards the supporting foot. (Although listed under 'One Sound' for convenience, this step includes as many sounds as desired, but with a minimum of two.)

3   Forward tap (fwd.tap)

Standing on one leg, the knee is bent and the working foot lifted slightly back. Swing the leg forward from the knee (with a small movement), allowing the ball of the foot to tap the ground en route.

The foot position before and after a straight tap.

Forward tap.
(1) The foot position before ...

(2) ... and after a forward tap.

4   Forward (fwd.brush)

The same sound and action as a forward tap, but the movement is slightly bigger.

5   Back tap (bk.tap)

The reverse of a forward tap, finishing with the foot held low at the back. Foot alignment should be parallel.

6   Back brush (bk.brush)

The same sound and action as back tap, but the movement is bigger. (The descriptions 'forward and back tap' and 'forward and back brush' are sometimes substituted for each other.)

7   Pick-up (pu) (also known as a 'spank')

Both feet on the ground with the working foot slightly forward. Lift the toe of the working foot and make a sharp slapping action backwards, hitting the ground with the ball of the foot as it passes through.

Pick-up.
(1) The foot position when the toe is released preparing for a pick-up ...

(2) ... the foot position after a pick-up.

8 Heel tap (heel-tap)
With the whole foot on the ground lift the heel, strike it on the ground and then immediately lift it again.

9 Ball tap (ball-tap)
The same as the heel tap, but using the ball of the foot.

10 Toe tap (toe-tap)
With the working leg bent and the foot held behind, and the thighs kept more or less together, strike the tip of the shoe on the ground and immediately lift. The instep should be extended to ensure clarity of tone, but the toes should not be clenched.

LEFT: Ball tap – the starting and finishing position.

RIGHT: Toe tap – the starting and finishing position.

Beats and Digs
A single sound made by the ball or the heel of the foot. The foot then remains on the ground and the sound is usually a heavier tone than the sound made in taps and brushes.

11 Ball beat (ball-beat)
The same movement as a ball tap, but the foot remains on the ground and the sound is heavier.

12 Heel beat (heelbt)
The same as a heel tap, but the foot remains on the ground and the sound is heavier.
13 Toe beat
The same as a toe tap, but the foot remains on the ground and the sound is heavier.
14 Toe beat drag
Execute a toe beat, and then drag the foot along the ground, thus prolonging the sound.
15 Drag
Can be taken with any part of the foot to prolong the sound of the preceding step.
16 Ball dig (ball-dig)
A heavy downward movement on to the ball of the foot. (This is usually taken without a transfer of weight.)
17 Touch
Similar to a ball dig, but the tone is lighter and the foot is lifted after the sound has been made.
18 Heel dig (heel-dig)
Lift the foot and make a firm downward movement on the underneath of the back edge of the heel.

Heel dig.
(1) The starting position ...
(2) ... the final position after placing the underneath of the heel on the ground.

Elevated Steps
19 Hop
Stand on one foot, hop, and land on the ball of the same foot, landing with the knee flexed. (Light tone.)
20 Jump
Stand on both feet with knees flexed. Jump into the air and land on the balls of both feet, flexing the knees (not a high jump – think of the action of jumping down a stair, rather than up it). (Light tone.)
21 Spring (also known as 'leap')
Stand on one foot, spring and land on the ball of the other foot with a fluid knee. (Light tone.)
22 Drop (version i) (drop.bll)
The same movement as spring, but by landing on a 'dry' knee the sound is heavier. (Medium tone.)
23 Drop (version ii) (drop.flt) (drop)
The same movement as version (i), but land on the whole foot, thus making a heavier sound than in version (i). The landing should be on the whole foot so that the quality and tone of the drop are the same as that of a stamp.

RIGHT: Drop on the ball of the foot – landing position.

FAR RIGHT: Drop on the flat of the foot – landing position.

OTHER STEPS MAKING ONE SOUND

24 Step
A transfer of weight on to the ball of the foot with a flexed knee. The sound should be light.

25 Stamp
Commence with the leg lifted and make a heavy sound on the *whole* foot. Students sometimes blur this sound. If so, lift the ball of the foot when preparing (so that the heel reaches the ground first), and eventually refine the movement so that the whole foot hits the ground together. (When the ball arrives first, a dull sound occurs.) To soften the tone, continue to bend the knee after the foot has hit the ground. A stamp can be taken with or without transfer of weight. (The stamp can be taken from any lifted position, e.g. behind, in front, or at the side of the supporting leg. Initially, however, the correct sound is more easily accomplished when taken from a lifted position in front.)

26 Stamp (w)
A stamp that is executed *with* a transfer of weight.

Stamp – if there is difficulty in achieving the correct sound, one way of practising is to lift the foot in front.
(1) Start with the leg lifted in front and the toes well lifted ...
(2) ... the whole foot should hit the ground at the same time.

27 Stamp (n) (sometimes called 'stomp')
A stamp in which the weight is *not* transferred.

28 Stomp (also called 'chug')
Stand on one foot with the other foot lifted behind – knee bent. Lift the heel of the supporting foot and slide or 'shunt' forwards on the ball making a clean sound with the heel. The movement should be small: a large movement will sacrifice clarity. (Medium or heavy tone.)

Note: In the exercises in this book the stomp will be the 'shunting' action described above (not the stamp).

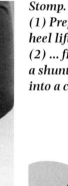

Stomp.
(1) Preparation with the heel lifted ...
(2) ... finishing position after a shunting action forward into a clean sound with heel.

Chug and Stomp

These steps are similar in movement. The chug usually describes the movement when both feet are on the ground and the stomp when one foot is lifted.

Chug.
(1) Lift the heel in preparation ...
(2) ... the finishing position of chug after a small slide forwards, finishing with a clean sound with the heel.

29 Chug (also known as 'travelling heel beat')
With both feet on the ground, release the heel of the working foot and slide it forwards on the ball, culminating with a sound of the heel (the same movement as a stomp). Sometimes taken in series on alternate feet, several on one foot, or both feet simultaneously. (Medium tone.)

30 Slam (also called flat stamp)

Similar to a stamp. However, it is taken with the working leg straight and lifted in front. The stamping sound is made with the leg stretched in front. The supporting leg is usually bent. (Medium tone.)

Slam.
(1) Lift foot in front to prepare ...
(2) ... hit the ground with the whole foot, the knee straight.

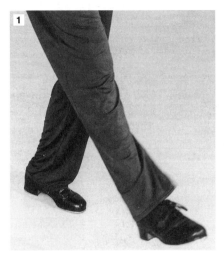 

31 Flat scuff (scuff(flt))

With the same leg action as a forward brush, the whole of the foot hits the ground as it swings forward. The sound should be the same as a stamp. (Heavy tone.)

Flat scuff.
(1) Starting position with foot lifted behind ...

(2) ... the whole foot hits the ground on the way forwards ...

(3) ... finishing with the leg extended forward.

Scuffs

Students often find difficulty in achieving clarity of tone in scuffs and stamps. In both, a dull, blurred tone sometimes occurs, especially if the ball of the foot hits the ground before the heel. Ideally the whole foot should strike the ground at once. However, if this is not possible initially, then it is infinitely better when the heel precedes the ball. Practise the stamp with the toe well lifted and the leg lifted in front. This position ensures that the heel meets the ground first, or (ideally) the whole foot hits simultaneously. Next, develop the movement to a scuff by bending the supporting leg during the preparation and straightening the knee to give clearance as the working foot is released forward.

32 Heel scuff ((hl) scuff)
The same leg action as a forward brush, but catch the underneath of the heel on the ground during the forward movement of the leg. (Medium tone.)

Heel scuff – at the point when the heel hits the ground.

Snatch.
(1) Prepare with pressure on the ball of the working foot ...

(2) ... the position of legs after the snatch.

33 Snatch
Place the working foot forward on the ball of the foot (with pressure). With one swift, rising movement, transfer the weight on to the back foot, simultaneously straightening the working leg and, with a *completely relaxed* working foot, allow the ball of the foot to slap the ground with a clean sound. (The tone is sharp, with extremely light or a medium tone.)

34 Heel clip (heel-clp)
Stand on both feet with bent knees. Lift the heels outward, and strike them together.

35 Toe clip (toe-clp)
The same as the heel clip, but lift the toes outwards and clip them together.

36 Toe-heel clip (toe-heel-clp)

Stand with one foot slightly forward. Lift the heel of the front foot and the whole back foot. Strike the toe against the heel of the supporting foot.

37 Heel-toe clip (heel-toe-clp)

The reverse of toe-heel clip.

38 Toe-heel clip travelling (toe-heel-clp.trav)

Toe of working foot hits heel of lifted supporting heel as it passes. Can be taken hitting the inside of the heel while the working foot is crossing behind or hitting the outside of the supporting heel before the working foot moves to an open position. (Usually followed by a step sideways.)

Two Sounds

39 Shuffles

The combination of a forward and back tap using a rhythm of less than two quarter notes. Shuffles are probably the most used step, and are extremely versatile. They can be taken in various positions, depending on the choreography of the combination. The basic shuffle is a straight shuffle. The tone is usually light, with a slightly stronger accent on the back tap if the rhythm 'a 1' is used. However, the level of tone can be altered to accommodate the rhythm required.

Technique of Shuffles

There are various opinions about the leg lines used for a shuffle. It has been said that the shuffle should not 'finish with the knee up in front' or that it should not 'finish with the foot behind'. All methods are valid, and in the final analysis it is the quality of the sound that is important. However, there are important differences in technical application. There is a method that, although the foot is relaxed, there is an element of control in the muscles of the foot. There is another in which the leg controls the movement, and the foot is completely relaxed.

40 Straight shuffle (str.shuffle)

Starting and finishing with the working foot lifted slightly behind the supporting foot. Take a forward and back tap in quick succession to a rhythm less than one beat (i.e. a1, +a, etc.). The foot hits the ground alongside the supporting foot during the forward and backward movements.

41 Side shuffle (sd.shuffle)

The working leg is taken to the side in a natural, slightly turned out line. There is an increase of bend in the supporting leg. The sound of the shuffle is made with the inside of the tap.

42 Back shuffle (bk.shuffle)

The working leg is taken behind, the bodyweight is held forward, and there is an increase of bend in the supporting leg. The shuffle is taken on the inside of the tap, with a natural 'turn-out'.

43 Lifted shuffle

Commence with the knee bent and lifted in front. The lower leg should hang vertically with the foot completely relaxed. Use a leg action down to hit the floor with a forward and back tap, and return the leg to the same lifted position.

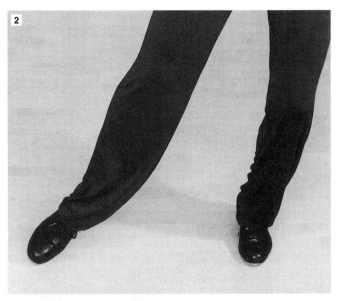

(1) Straight shuffle, the starting and finishing position.

(2) Side shuffle, the starting and finishing position.

(3) Back shuffle, the starting and finishing position.

(4) Shuffle in front, the starting and finishing position.

Playing with Shuffles

For a choreography, a dancer should be able to shuffle in any position in order to accommodate the movement and style of the sequence. For this reason it is useful to practise 'Around the clock' shuffles. Think of the supporting foot standing where the hands join in the centre, and then take the working foot from 12 o'clock, to 1 o'clock, 2 o'clock, 3 o'clock, 4 o'clock and 5 o'clock. The bodyweight and the degree of bend in the supporting knee will be adjusted to accommodate the execution of the shuffle.

44 Shuffle across the supporting foot (shuffle.Xf)

Commence with the foot lifted behind. Take a forward tap. The back tap is taken across the front of the supporting leg.

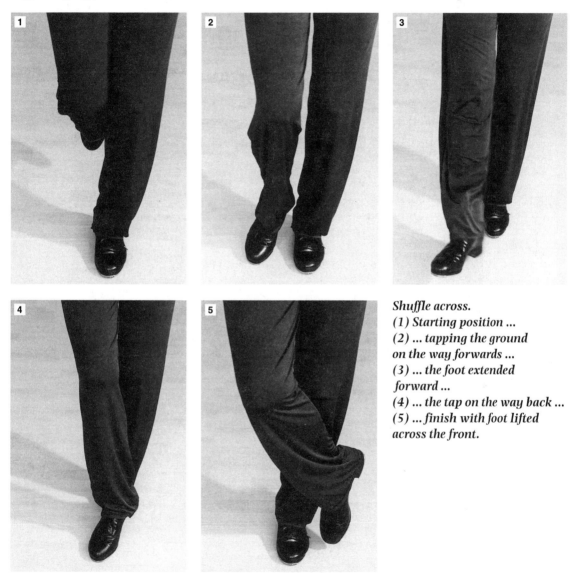

Shuffle across.
(1) Starting position ...
(2) ... tapping the ground on the way forwards ...
(3) ... the foot extended forward ...
(4) ... the tap on the way back ...
(5) ... finish with foot lifted across the front.

45 Flap

Lift the working leg behind, and make one floppy movement forwards, executing a forward tap and a step on the ball (or the whole) of the foot. The leg controls the action, and the foot should be completely relaxed so that the sounds produced are very close together (brm). When first practising, the emphasis should be on achieving the relaxation rather than concentrating on making the sounds. If the foot action is correct, the clarity of tone will follow.

46 Tap step (tp.step) (also sometimes called flap)

Forward tap and step. It is similar to a flap, but the action has more control in the foot and, therefore, a different rhythmic quality (e.g. a1.).

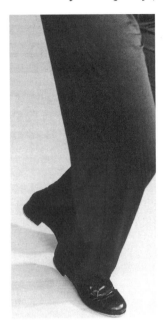 

FAR LEFT: **Tap step, finishing position.**

LEFT: **Tap spring, finishing position.**

47 Tap spring (also known as 'running flap')

Commence with the working foot lifted at the back. Execute a forward tap and a spring on the working foot. Think of it as one movement only. Both the tap and the spring should be executed while the body is on the way down. This is the best way to achieve the ideal rhythm of accented eighths. (*Note:* In the running flaps the lifted leg is lower than in tap spring.)

Tap Step and Flap	Tap Steps and Tap Springs
Some dancers use the word 'flap' for both the 'tap-step' and the 'flap', but using a slightly different pronunciation for each to differentiate the rhythm: thus the former would become 'ferlap', and the latter remain 'flap'.	The two steps are similar. To differentiate, think of the former as a walking step and the latter as a running movement.

48 Ball change (bll.chge)

Step RF: step LF: taken to less than the count of 1, 2. Either ball to ball (bll.chge) or ball to flat (bll.chge(flt)). The knees should be flexed. (Technically, the first step is taken behind, and the second in front. However, the foot position depends on the choreography.)

49 Step heel-beat (step-heelbt)

A step and a heel beat. In its simplest form it would be taken as two movements to the counts 1, 2. (It is also a useful step for close work or rhythm tap.) (*See* 128.)

Step heel-beat.
(1) Step of step heel-beat with weight forward ...
(2) ... heel-beat of step heel-beat.

50 Heel-dig ball-beat (heel-ball)

A heel dig followed by a ball beat. Do not transfer the weight until the ball beat.

51 Pick-up step (pu step)

A pick-up; a step back with a clean sound on to the ball of the working foot.

52 Pick-up change (pu.chge) (*see* illustrations overleaf)

Stand on the RF with the LF lifted behind. Spring into the air, but before leaving the ground momentarily, lift the ball of the right foot. Execute a back tap (or pick-up) whilst springing up, and then land on the ball of the left foot with the knee flexed. This will produce two sounds. Sufficient elevation should be applied to ensure separation of the sounds and clarity of tone. To begin with it is a good idea to practise this step while using the support of 'the barre' or a chair.

53 Pick-up on one foot (pu.1.ft)

Stand on the right foot with the left leg lifted behind. Then execute the same movement as in a pick-up change, but land on the ball of the right foot. There is no change of foot in this step. The step will travel slightly backwards, and there should be sufficient elevation to separate the sounds. (Initially to be practised at the barre or with support.)

Alternative Names and Preparatory Exercises

Name: Some dancers refer to pick-up change and/or pick-up on one foot as pull-backs. However, pull-backs, when used in the ensuing chapters, will be those producing four sounds (*see* 99 and 100).

Preparation: A good way to prepare for these steps is to execute the movement of pick-up on one foot with both feet simultaneously, preceded by a jump. This preparation could be taken sitting on a chair, holding on to a barre, or without any support.

Pick-up change (see *No. 52, previous page*).

(1) Prepare standing on RF – both knees bent ...

(2) ... lift the toe of the RF ...

(3) ... spring into the air executing the pick-up ...

(4) ... prepare to land on the LF ...

(5) ... land on the ball of the foot ...

(6) ... continue to flex the knee on landing.

54 Snatch back (sntch.bk)

This is like a flap in reverse. Take a snatch and then step. The foot must be completely relaxed, just as in the snatch.

55 Scuffle
Forward tap, heel dig RF transferring the weight on to the R heel.
(Usually preceded by a step.)

56 Reverse scuffle (rev.scuffle)
Heel dig RF (without weight), ball dig RF (with transfer of weight).
Usually preceded by a step.

57 Hop heel (2s.hop)
A two-sounded hop. Execute a hop, landing first ball and then heel, all in one movement so that the two sounds are very close to each other.

58 Spring heel (2s.spring)
The same as hop heel, but changing feet.

THREE SOUNDS

59 Tap-step heel beat
The same movement as a tap step, and then add a heel beat. The transfer of weight occurs on the second sound, i.e. the step.

60 Tap heel ball
Forward tap, heel dig, ball beat. The weight is transferred on the final sound.

Scuffle, finishing position with the weight on the heel.

61 Pick-up hop step
A combination of a pick-up, a hop, and a step backwards.

62 Pick-up spring step
A combination of a pick-up, a spring, and a step backwards.

63 Pick-up ball change (pu bll.chge)
(Usually taken turning.) A combination of a pick-up and a ball change (ball to ball). After the first step of the ball change (and during the second step of the ball change) the foot preparing for the next pick-up should be rolled sensitively on to the heel ready for a repeat. No sound should occur from the heel during this transition. It is a useful exercise to develop sensitivity of foot action.

64 Shuffle spring
(bk) Shuffle RF: spring RF (bringing foot underneath body): repeat LF. Can also be taken using a side shuffle. The rhythm should be smooth to twelfth notes (& a 1 & a 2 etc.).

65 Clip-ball-change
(Similar to a galloping action.) Stand with the feet apart and the weight on the right foot. Travelling to the right, spring into the air clipping the left foot to the right foot (the sides of the shoes hitting to make the clipping sound); land on the ball of the left foot, and then the ball of the right foot. A repeat would continue in the same direction.

Clip-ball-change: position in the air at the moment of the clip.

66 Three-sound shuffle (3s.shuffle)
(also known as an open third or three-beat shuffle)
The same foot action as a two-sound shuffle, but allowing the heel of the working foot to hit the ground at the climax of the forward movement. All three sounds are usually taken within one beat. The foot must be relaxed, and the movement should be controlled by the leg action.

67 Three-sound flap (3s.flap) (also known as a closed third or three-beat flap)

The same actions as a two-sound flap, but after the forward tap, allow the heel to catch the ground before lowering the ball of the foot. The working foot must be completely relaxed. The movement is controlled by the leg action. (This can be taken with or without transfer of weight.)

FOUR SOUNDS

68 Double shuffle

Two shuffles taken speedily with minimal leg action. The foot should be relaxed. These can be taken in any direction (i.e. front, side, back, around the clock).

69 Tap-step ball change

Tap-step RF ball change L R (back front). Keep the movement well contained. Travel forwards, side to side, or turning.

70 Shuffle hop step (also known as 'Irish')

(Straight) shuffle RF: hop LF: step RF back: or travel forwards with (side) shuffle RF: hop LF: step. RF across the front.

71 Shower flap (also known as 'double flap')

Two flaps performed with tight rhythm, e.g. 'nna1'. Ideally the step is achieved by springing up and lifting both feet back and off the ground simultaneously. Then take a flap on the right, followed immediately by a flap on the left.

MORE STEPS

Riffs and Riff Walks

72 Open riff forwards (two sounds) (2s.open.riff.fwd)

The same leg action as a forward brush, but catching first the ball, and then the tip of the heel on the ground. Finish with the leg raised in front – knee straight. One flowing movement with no jerkiness or hesitation.

73 Open riff backwards (two sounds) (2s.open.riff.bk)

The same leg action as a back brush, but hitting first the tip of the heel and then the ball of the foot on the ground. Finish with the leg raised at the back. As in the open riff forwards, this should be one flowing leg action.

74 Open riff forwards (three sounds) (3s.open.riff.fwd or 3 beat riff forward)

Execute a two-sound open riff forwards, and then a heel beat with the supporting foot. Finish with the leg raised in front – the knee straight (but not stiff). The movement comes from the knee. There should be no increase in height during the heel beat.

75 Open riff backwards (three sounds) (3s.open.riff.bk or 3 beat riff back)

As in two-sound open riff backwards, but add a heel beat on the supporting foot.

Riff Walks

There should be no jerkiness or hesitation in the movement of a riff walk. The leg action should be one smooth movement, and the sounds executed as the foot passes through. When practising, concentrate initially on the walking action, and allow clarity of sound to develop later.

76 Four-sound riff (4s.riff) (also known as riff walk or four-beat riff)

Execute a two-sound open riff forwards, followed by heel dig, ball beat on the working foot. The weight is transferred on the final ball beat.

Riff walk: there should be one smooth, continuous action in this step.
(1) Starting position, the foot lifted behind and making a fluid movement of the leg
(2) ... tap the ground with the ball of the foot ...

(3) ... catch the heel on the ground ...

(4) ... extend the leg forwards with the knee straight but not tense ...

(5) ... heel dig ...

(6)... ball beat, transferring the weight.

77 Five-sound riff (5s.riff) (also known as riff walk or five-beat riff)

Execute a three-sound open riff followed by heel dig, ball beat on the working foot. The weight is transferred on the final ball beat.

78 Six-sound riff (6s.riff) (also known as riff walk or six-beat riff)

Execute a five-sound riff and add a heel beat on the front foot. (The weight should be transferred on the fifth sound.)

79 Seven-sound riff (7s.riff) (also known as riff walk or seven-beat riff)
Execute a five-sound riff, and then add a heel beat on the back foot, followed by a heel beat on the front foot. (The weight should not be transferred until the seventh sound.)

80 Eight-sound riff (8s.riff) (also known as riff walk)
Execute a seven-sound riff, and add a ball beat on the front foot at the end. (The weight should not be transferred until the final ball beat.)

(Alternative combinations of sounds could be used to achieve the various riffs. For example, a five-sound riff can also be taken as a four-sound riff, but adding a heel beat on the working foot at the end. However, the above examples are usual.)

81 Criss-cross riff (x.x.riff)
An open three-sound riff forwards; an open three-sound riff back (and across working leg); a forward riff (either four, five, six or seven sounds, thus creating a ten-, eleven-, twelve- or thirteen-sound criss-cross riff).

(Criss-cross riffs can also be taken with an open two-sound riff forwards and backwards, and any desired number of sounds in the forward riff.)

Hopping Riffs

82 Five-sound hopping riff (5s.hopping riff)
The same as an ordinary riff, but substitute a hop for the heel beat.

83 Six-sound hopping riff (6s.hopping riff)
The same as a 6s.riff, but substitute hop for the first heel beat.

84 Seven-sound hopping riff (7s.hopping riff)
The same as a 7s.riff, but substitute a hop for the first heel beat, i.e. two-sound open riff forward RF, hop LF, heel-dig, ball-beat RF, heel-beat LF, heel-beat RF.

Hop-Heel Riffs

85 Six-sound hop-heel riff (6s.hop-heel riff)
Execute a two-sound open-riff forward RF, 2s.hop LF (*see* number 57), heel-dig ball-beat RF.

86 Seven-sound hop-heel riff (7s.hop-heel riff)
Execute a two-sound open-riff forward RF, 2s.hop LF (*see* number 57), heel-dig ball-beat, heel beat RF.

87 Eight-sound hop-heel riff (8s.hop-heel riff)
Execute a two-sound open-riff forward RF, 2s.hop LF (*see* number 57), heel-dig ball-beat RF, heel beat LF, heel beat RF.

Cramp Rolls

88 Four-sound cramp roll (4s.crmp rl) (also known as four-beat cramp roll)
A jumping action. Spring into the air with the legs straight and underneath body. Land on ball of RF then ball of LF, followed by heel of RF and heel of LF. There should be a fluid action of the knees on landing. The resulting rhythm should have a rippling quality, with the sounds separated but as close together as possible. Think of the final heel beat arriving on the beat of the music. The remainder of the sound should be just before it in a 'cluster' – a sort of 'brrm'.

(The four-beat cramp roll can also be taken with a controlled action, resulting in a rhythm such as '+1+2' or 'e+a1'.)

89 Five-sound cramp roll (5s.crmp rl) (also known as five-beat cramp roll)
Lift the RF behind. Tap spring RF: step LF: heel beat RF: heel beat LF. Finish with relaxed knees. (Unlike the 4s.crmp rl, the 5s. has controlled rhythm, e.g. a1& a2.)

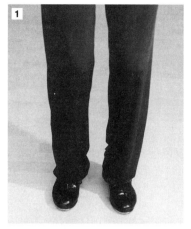

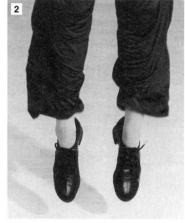

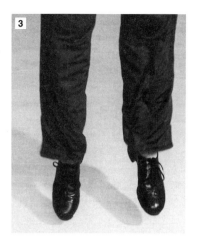

4s. cramp roll.
(1) Preparation with the knees bent ...
(2) ... jump with straight knees in the air ...
(3) ... land on the ball of the RF ...
(4) ... land on the ball of the LF ...
(5) ... heel-beat R and heel-beat L.

5s.cramp roll.
(1) Prepare with RF behind ...

(2) ... tap spring RF releasing LF

(3) ... step LF into heel-beats R and L.

90 Six-sound crmp rl (6s.crmp rl) (also known as the six-beat cramp roll)

Lift the right foot behind. Tap spring RF: tap step LF: heel beat RF: heel beat LF. Finish with relaxed knees.

6s.cramp roll.
(1) Prepare with RF lifted behind ...

(2) ... tap spring R, lifting L behind ...

(3) ... tap step L ...

(4)... heel-beats R and L.

91 Cramp-roll change (crmp-rl.chge)

Four, five or six beats. The same action as the normal (or regular) cramp rolls, but the heel beats are taken in reverse order.

92 Shuffle cramp roll (five sounds) (sh.crmp.rl.5s)

Stand on LF. Side shuffle with RF: ball-dig heel-beat RF at side of LF: heel beat LF.

93 Shuffle cramp roll (six sounds) (sh.crmp.rl.6s)

Stand on LF: side shuffle RF; four-beat cramp roll RF.

94 Turning cramp roll (trng.crmp.rl)

A normal (or regular) four-sound cramp roll RF (making one complete turn to R).

95 Turning cramp-roll change (trng.crmp.rl.chge)

This is usually preceded by a step, e.g. step RF: cramp-roll change LF. (Make one complete turn to right. Use a 4s. or 5s. cramp roll.)

96 Press cramp roll (four sounds)

Lift the RF up in front. Heel beat LF: lower the RF with one action, making a sound with the ball and the heel; while lifting the RF up in front, take another heel beat on the LF. The sound is a 'cluster' e.g. 'nna1'.

97 Standing cramp roll

Shuffle RF: step heel-beat RF (beside LF): heel dig LF.

Pull-Backs

98 Pull-back (taken from the whole foot) (also known as double pull-back)

Having already learned nos 7 and 52, stand with RF slightly forward and the weight on the back foot, both heels down. Pick-up RF: pick-up change L to R: step back LF. (Whilst in the air the knees are bent.) The natural rhythm for a pull-back is the 'cluster', i.e. 'nna1'.

Press cramp roll.
(1) Prepare with RF lifted and make a heel-beat with LF ...

(2) ... with a leg action and a relaxed foot, take a ball and heel sound with RF ...

(3) ... heel-beat on LF, lifting the RF to starting position.

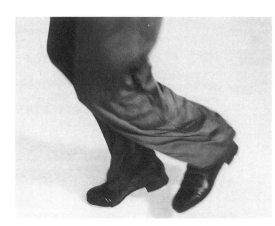

ABOVE: The landing of a pull-back (taken from the whole foot) – both knees are bent whilst in the air.

RIGHT: Pull-back from the balls of the feet, both knees stretched whilst in the air.

Pull-Backs from the Whole Foot and from the Balls of the Feet

These two steps, although similar, require a different technique to each other (as seen from the descriptions). Each has its own advantage: those from the whole foot (no. 98) can be taken with a 'cluster' rhythm, i.e. 'nna1', or with controlled rhythm, e.g. 'e+a1' or '1&a2'. The pull-backs from the balls of the feet (no. 99) are always danced to the 'cluster' rhythm, i.e. 'nna1'. However, the advantage is that they can be executed with greater speed and lighter tone. No. 98 is easier to master than no. 99. However, the one does not necessarily help with learning the other.

99 Pull-back (taken from balls of feet) (sntch.pull-back)

Having already learned no. 33, stand on the balls of both feet, RF forward (with pressure). Execute a snatch on the RF, followed by a pick-up change with a snatching action from the ball of the foot. Both snatches occur on the way up. (Whilst in the air, both knees are *straight* and the feet are completely relaxed.) The natural rhythm is a cluster i.e. 'nna1'.

100 Open and closed pull-backs (opn.&.clsd.pll-bk)
These pull-backs are taken on the balls of the feet with the snatching action. Commence with feet apart (sideways), and then execute a series of pull-backs, alternately bringing the feet together and then apart.

101 Tip-top pull-back
These require a lot of elevation and should not be confused with 'toe stands'. From both feet, jump and, whilst suspended, execute a toe tap with the RF and then the LF. Land on the ball of the RF, followed by a step on the LF. The four sounds should be cleanly separated but in a cluster, like grace notes.

Shuffle Pick-Up Changes

102 Shuffle pick-up change (also known as crawl)
Stand on one foot with bodyweight forward. Take a back shuffle, followed by a pick-up change. The step has four sounds and the natural rhythm is 'e+a1'. Add a heel beat to make five sounds (e+na1).

103 Double-shuffle pick-up change
The same as a shuffle pick-up change, but at the beginning, execute a double shuffle instead of a shuffle. (Shuffle pick-up change and double-shuffle pick-up change can also be taken with the 'snatch' action.)

Ripples

104 Three-sound ripple (3s.ripple) (also known as three-beat ripple)
Forward tap followed by pick-up change. The forward tap has minimal movement, and the action must be similar to a tap spring with the weight over the balls of the feet.

105 Four-sound ripple (4s.ripple) (also known as four-beat ripple)
The same as a three-sound ripple, but add a heel beat at the end.

106 Rippledown
A three-sound ripple followed immediately with a step behind. (The action must feel like one movement and be taken within one beat of music.)
Note: Numbers 98 to 106 all require sufficient elevation to separate the sounds.

CLOG WALTZ (OR WALTZ CLOG) (ALSO KNOWN AS BASIC WALTZ)

107 Single waltz (side to side)
Spring RF (slightly sideways): (sd) shuffle LF: ball change (bk.fr L R): (count '1+2+3').

108 Single waltz (foot in front) (sngl waltz(fr))
Spring RF (slightly forward); shuffle L(XfR); ball change (LR with L in front of R).

109 Single Waltz (foot behind) (sngl waltz(b))
Spring RF (slightly forward); (str) shuffle LF: ball change L R (with L behind R and a slight turn of body to R).

110 Double waltz
As in all single waltz sequences, but commencing with a tap spring (counts '+1+2+3').

Wings

111 Mock wing (also known as fake wing, or preparation wing)
Stand with the feet together and the knees bent. Straighten the legs, and at the same time release the right foot to the side with a scraping sound. As the right foot returns, make a tap and then a step, finishing with both knees bent. (A supported wing is similar, taken with the left foot in toe-beat position at the back. Leave the left toe on the ground whilst executing the wing.)

(Having learned the preparation, the easiest progression would be to try the double wing. However, for simplicity, the single wing analyses are notated next.)

112 Single wing three sounds (3s.sngl.wing) (also known as three-beat single wing)
This is the same movement as that in the 'preparation' or 'Mock' wing, but executed from one foot only with the other foot lifted behind.

113 Single wing four sounds (4s.sngl.wing) (four-beat single wing)
As in a single wing, but add either a heel beat with the working foot, or a toe-tap at the back with the free foot. (The single wing with the toe tap could be performed with the toe tap first in front and then behind – rather like a cutaway action.)

114 Single wing five sounds (5s.sngl.wing) (five-beat single wing)
The same as the single wing, but add both the heel beat and the toe tap.

A Five-Sound Wing Making all the Sounds with the Working Foot

Frank Condos was one of the few people ever to achieve a five-sound wing. However, this was not the five-sound wing described in the vocabulary: he did it by using just the right amount of elevation, and adding more sounds with the winging foot! With a relaxed working foot he would make one sound (scrape) with the hopping foot on the way out and then four on the way down. Paul Draper achieved four sounds on one foot – scrape out and shuffle step on the way down. Sam Weber achieved five sounds: his was with a scrape out and then (with a relaxed foot) another sound on the way out and a shuffle step on the way down. All remarkable feats!

115 Change wing three sounds (3s.chge.wing) (three-beat change wing)
As in a single wing with three sounds, but land on the opposite foot.

116 Change wing four sounds (4s.chge.wing) (four-beat change wing)
As in the single wing with four sounds, but change feet.

117 Change wing five sounds (5s.chge.wing) (five-beat change wing)
As in the single wing with five sounds, but change feet.

118 Double wing three sounds (3s.dbl wing) (three-beat double wing)
Start with feet together, knees bent and heels lifted. Execute the same foot action as the single wing, but with both feet simultaneously.

119 Double wing four or five sounds (4s. and 5s.dbl wing)
The same as a double wing, but add one or two heel beats at the end.

120 Separated wing (sep.wing)
The same as a double wing, but start one foot before the other. Finish one foot and then finish the other. It should make at least five sounds.

121 Wing combined with shuffle ball dig
A single wing on one foot while the free foot executes a shuffle and a ball dig.

122 Pendulum wing
The same as a single wing, but the working leg does a forward and back brush. Ideally it should be the brush and then the wing. However, the wing could be taken first, followed by the brush.

123 Butterfly wing
The same as a double wing, but make a half circular action whilst travelling backwards. This is often an easier way to start learning wings.

CLOSE WORK

124 Paddle and roll (also known as paddle)

Heel dig (at side or in front); pick-up (towards supporting leg): step heel beat: all with the right foot. Repeat the whole with the left foot. The rhythm should be even. Take even 8ths (1+2+) for practice. Gradually increase the speed, and then use 16th notes (1e+a2e+a). The first two sounds are the 'paddle', and the step and heel beat are the 'roll'.

Paddle and roll with the foot action forward. (1) Heel-dig with RF ...

(2) ... pick-up with RF ...

(3) ... step on to RF ...

(4) ... heel-beat RF, releasing LF for repeat.

Paddle and roll, with foot action at the side. (1) Heel-dig to the side with RF ...

(2) ... foot returns after pick-up ...

(3) ... step on to RF ...

(4) ... heel-beat RF, immediately releasing LF for repeat.

125 Double paddle and roll
(or double paddle) (dbl.paddle)

Heel dig (front or side): pick-up: heel dig: pick-up (towards supporting leg): step heel beat.

126 Paddle break (pdle.brk)

Paddle and roll RF: step heel beat LF; paddle and roll (RF); step heel beat (LF); paddle and roll (RF).

127 Five-sound paddle (5s.paddle)

Forward tap, heel dig (to front or to side): pick-up (towards supporting leg): step heel beat.

Close Work (a.k.a. Rhythm Tap)

The foot action should be small and close to the ground. Elevated steps are rarely used – but when included, they barely clear the floor. Maximize the number of sounds made with each foot action and minimize the number of weight changes within a sequence. Heel beats and chugs are amongst the few single-sound steps suitable for speed. Some useful steps are: paddles, rattles, step heel-beat, tap step heel-beat, and shuffle step heel-beat.

5s. Paddle and roll.
(1) Prepare with RF lifted ...
(2) ... forward tap ...
(3) ... heel-dig ...
(4) ... pick-up ...
(5) ... lift after pick-up ...
(6) ... step RF beside LF ...
(7) ... heel-beat RF, releasing LF ready for repeat.

Step-heel as close work.
(1) Prepare, lifting RL with a completely relaxed foot ...
(2) ... step-heel, all in one movement, releasing LF for repeat.

Ball-heel turn.
(1) Prepare with step RF across LF ...
(2) ... start to turn making a heel-beat with RF ...
(3) ... continue turning, making heel-beat with LF whilst releasing ball of RF ...
(4) ... continue turning, executing ball-beat with RF and releasing ball of LF ...
(5) ... complete the turn with a ball-beat on the LF.

128 Step heel beat (as a close-work step) (step heel)

To make 'step heel-beat' effective as a close-work step it should be taken as one movement. To achieve this, keep the foot completely relaxed, lift the leg, and then put the foot down making one movement so that the two sounds follow each other immediately. Take in a series, and practice to gradually increase the speed; they can eventually sound similar to machine guns. (The same action as the roll of paddle and roll.)

129 Ball-heel turn

Commence with RF across (close) in front of LF. Make a twist turn to the left, and at the same time execute heel beats R L followed by ball beats R L. This step can be done with any combination of ball beats and heel beats, turning in either direction. It can also be preceded by an open 2s. riff forward and an open 2s. riff across in front of supporting leg.

130 Single travel (sngl.trav)

Stand with the weight on one foot (the other can be lifted or remain on the ground without weight). Travel sideways on one foot with ball beat (turning foot out): heel beat (turning foot in).

131 Double travel (dbl.trav)

Stand on both feet, feet slightly apart. Ball beat RF (turning foot out); ball beat LF (turning foot in); heel beat RF (turning foot in); heel beat LF (turning foot out); continue in same directions for as long as desired. Can be taken in either direction, or with feet moving away from, and towards each other.

132 Cahito or draw-back (dr.bk)

Pick-up RF: heel beat LF: step RF. Can also be taken with a chug instead of the heel beat.

133 Bambalina (or Cincinnati)

Pick-up RF: heel beat LF: (sd)shuffle RF: step (RF back). A hop can be substituted for the heel beat.

134 Rattle

Tap-step heel-beat fwd. RF: toe tap LF: heel beat RF: step back LF: pick-up step RF(tog): shuffle step LF: shuffle RF: ball change RL: heel beat LF. Footwork should be kept very small throughout. No increase of height during the heel beats. The natural rhythm is 'e+a1e+a2e+a3e+a4'. When first learning it could be practised to '+8+1+2+3+4+5+6+7'.

135 Progressive rattle (prog.rattle)

Tap-step heel-beat fwd. RF: toe tap LF: heel beat RF: step back LF: pick-up step RF(tog): shuffle step LF: shuffle RF: 4s.cramp roll. The footwork should be kept very small throughout. There should be no increase of height during the heel beats. The natural rhythm is 'e+a1e+a2e+a3e+na4'.

136 Double toe-tap rattle

Tap-step heel-beat fwd. RF: toe tap LF: heel beat RF: toe tap LF: heel beat RF: step back LF: pick-up step RF(tog): shuffle step LF: shuffle RF: ball change RL: heel beat LF. The footwork should be kept very small throughout. There should be no increase of height during the heel beats. The natural rhythm is 'e+a1e+a2e+a3e+a4e+'.

137 Double toe-tap progressive rattle (dbl.toe-tap prog.rattle)

Tap-step heel-beat fwd. RF: toe tap LF: heel beat RF: toe tap LF: heel beat RF: step back LF: pick-up step RF(tog): shuffle step LF: shuffle RF: 4s.cramp roll RF. The footwork should be kept very small throughout. There should be no increase of height during the heel-beats. The natural rhythm is 'e+a1e+a2e+a3e+a4en+'.

EXTRA STEPS

Most of the following steps require a completely relaxed foot, the control coming either from the knee or the hip.

138 Flam (outside) and flam (inside); (abbreviation: flam(outs) and flam(ins))

The step can be taken on the outside of the foot or the inside of the shoe.

(a) Outside: Cross the RF over the left foot with the sole of the foot lifted to face the side. Hit the foot on the floor, making a sound first with the edge of the toe and then the edge of the heel. The rhythm is like a grace note in music. Count would be 'n1 ... n2' etc.

(b) Inside: Take the RF to the side and hit the ground with the inside of the shoe, first the toe and then the heel. (Flam is a drummer's word for 'grace notes'.)

Flam (on the outside of the foot).
(1) repare with RF XfL ...
(2) ... hit the ground with the outside of the sole of the shoe ...
(3) ... hit the ground with the outside of the heel of the shoe.
(4) Flam (on the inside of foot). Hold RL to RS. First, hit the inside of the sole of the shoe on the ground ...
(5) ... then hit the inside of the heel of the shoe on the ground.

SHUFFLES

139 Undercut Shuffle

Stand on the left foot. Take the right foot in close behind the left, and using the outside edge of the shoe take a shuffle action. Make three sounds: first, moving the foot forward, hit the outside edge of the ball and then the heel – then immediately move the foot back, making another sound with the side of the ball. The foot action is similar to that of the three-sound shuffle.

Undercut shuffle. (1) Prepare with RF behind ...

(2) ... take RF forward (on other side of LF), making a sound with the outside of the sole of the shoe ...

(3) ... continue RF forward making a sound with the outside of the heel of the shoe ...

(4) ... take the foot back again, making a sound with the outside of the sole of the shoe.

140 2 tap shuffle forward

Swing the leg forward with a completely relaxed foot; stretch the knee at the end of the movement. The ball of the floppy foot will catch the floor and then, in its relaxed mode, rebound and catch the floor again as the knee straightens.

141 3 tap shuffle (or 3tap shuffle-brush)

Take the 2t.shuffle forward as described above, and then immediately after the stretch, bend and lift the knee in front, allowing the ball of the relaxed foot to catch the floor on the way back.

142 3 tap shuffle fwd (using ball and heel of foot)

Take a brush forward. Keep the foot relaxed. As the leg moves forwards, catch the ball of the foot, then the heel and then the ball again on the ground. Finish with a stretched knee.

143 4 tap shuffle forward (ball, heel, heel ball)

Swing the leg forward catching first the ball; the heel; then the heel again on the rebound; and then the ball. Can be finished off the ground, or it can finish on the ground like a flap. The four sounds should be completed within one beat or less.

144 Side riff (three sounds) (also known as a side shuffle)

The foot will move sideways away from, and then towards the supporting foot. With the widest part of the tap (of the ball), flick the foot out and catch the outside of the tap; flick it back towards the supporting foot catching the inside of the tap; then catch the underneath of the tap. The three sounds should be completed within one beat or less, and are all made while the foot is moving forwards.

145 Eddie Brown's double third

This step uses heel beats and 3s.shuffles (or riffle) (*see* no. 66). The action is similar to a press cramp roll (no. 96). It consists of a heel beat LF: 3s.shuffle RF: heel beat LF.

146 Shuffle ripple

Shuffle on the right combined with a pick-up on one foot on the left foot. However, the feet alternate. The order of the sounds is the first sound of the shuffle (with the right foot moving forwards); the first sound of the pick-up on one foot (springing into the air and making the pick-up sound); the back tap of the shuffle; then the land from the pick-up on one foot. It could be described as 'Shuf- pu- fle – land'. This can also be done changing feet, using a pick-up change.

(With thanks to Sam Weber for the notes on numbers 138 to 146)

147 Reverse Cramp Roll

Spring on to R heel (heel-dig action): step on to L heel (heel dig action) (feet slightly apart): step on to ball of RF: step on to ball of LF: (feet together). The movement is quick and produces a similar rhythm to the four-sound cramp roll – count 'nna1' or 'nnna'.

CLIP PULL-BACKS

148 Clip pull-back on one foot (four sounds) (clp.pll.bk.1.ft.4s)

Stand on both feet, with RF slightly forward. Execute a pick-up with the RF; make the first sound of a pick-up on one foot (no. 53), but before landing, clip the side of the RF against the side of the LF, i.e. pickup – pull – clip – land. The clip could be toe to heel or the sides of the feet.

149 Clip pull-back on one foot (five sounds) (clp.pll.bk.1.ft.5s)

As in four sounds, but add a heel beat.

150 Clip pull-back change (four sounds) (clp.pll.bk.chge.4s)

The same movements as in clip pull-back on one foot, but change feet to land.

151 Clip pull-back change (five sounds) (clp.pll.bk.chge.5s)

As in four sounds, but add a heel beat.

152 Clip double pull-back (five sounds) (clp.dbl.pll.bk.1.ft.5s)

The same action as pull-back (nos 98 and 99), but add a clip of the sides of the feet between the first two sounds.

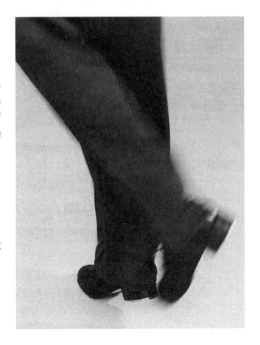

Clip-pull-back, the moment just after the clip.

6 TRADITIONAL STEPS AND TIME-STEPS

Many traditional steps and combinations, such as maxi-fords, falling off the log, over the top, pulling the trenches and essences, have become part of the tap-dancers' vocabulary. Some are listed in the following chapter.

Time-steps were originally used as a method of setting the tempo – thus 'time-step'. In the days of vaudeville, music hall and touring shows, rehearsal time was minimal. In order to establish the tempo required, a dancer would commence with one of the traditional time-steps because the rhythm was clearly defined and the speed easily recognized by the musicians. The dancer could then, if he wished, progress safely to a variety of complex rhythms.

Time-steps are often used as an aid to perfect rhythm, timing and tone quality – rather like scales on the piano. They are arranged in short phrases (one bar or two bars), are simple and repetitive, and most can be developed from a single to a double or a triple variation. There is always a break at the end of a series of time-steps: it literally 'breaks the monotony' of the sequence. The usual format fits into an eight-bar phrase, comprising six (or two) time-steps, and a break taking two bars.

This chapter includes some of the many traditional as well as some choreographed time-steps. For each type of time-step there is a 'comfortable' dancing tempo: for instance, ragtime is useful for shuffle time-steps; swing or straight timing suits off-beat and pick-up time-steps.

Exercise to stretch the backs of the legs.

Developing Expressive Tone

Use the traditional and time step sequences to practise rhythm and develop tone. Be aware of the light sounds, such as taps, brushes, hops and springs, and the heavy sounds, such as stamps, stomps, scuffs, beats and digs. Use their natural weight to produce the relevant level of sound; but within each category create variation in the tone so that, in addition to light and heavy sounds, there will be 'shades of grey'. The rhythm of each combination should contain expression. Remember to warm-up properly, to stretch out the backs of the legs and to keep the feet relaxed but sensitive.

SOME TRADITIONAL AND SOME COMBINATION STEPS

Maxi-Ford

Maxi-Ford (with toe tap) (M/F(w.toe.tap)

The counting of this step is tricky. One way to master the rhythm is to note the step being done on the actual counts 1 2 3 4 etc., and then fit the other sounds in between. There are two ways it could be counted, depending on the speed of the music being used; for simplicity the second is the easier of the two methods.

For a slow to medium tempo: 1 e + n a 2 + a 3 e + n 4 + 5 e + n a 6 + a 7 e n + 8

For a quick tempo count half time: 1 a 2 + a 3 4 a 5 + a 6 7 8 1 a 2 + a 3 4 a 5 + a 6 7

R	L	(R to L)	R	R	L	(R to L)	R	R	L

Drop: shuffle: pu.chge: toe tap: **Drop**: shuffle: pu.chge: toe tap: 2 low runs (balls of feet)

<u>1</u>	e +	n a	2	±	a 3	e n	+	4	+
<u>1</u>	a 2	+ a	3	<u>4</u>	a 5	+ a	6	7	8

---

153 Maxi-ford with toe tap – without pick-up

(The drop is on the whole foot)

R		L	L	R	R	L	L	R	R	L

Drop(flt): shuffle: spring: toe tap: drop(flt): shuffle: spring: toe tap: run: run:

<u>1</u>		+ 2	+	3	<u>4</u>	+ 5	+	6	7	8

R		L	L	R	R	L	L	R	R

Drop(flt): shuffle: spring: toe tap: drop(flt): shuffle: spring: toe tap: run.

<u>1</u>		+ 2	+	3	<u>4</u>	+ 5	+	6	7

Or with a pick-up change

R	L	R to L	R	R	L	R to L	R	R	L

Drop(flt): shuffle: pu.chge: toe tap: drop(flt): shuffle: pu.chge: toe tap: run: run:

1	a 2	+ a	3	4	a 5	+ a	6	7	8

R	L	R to L	R	R	L	R to L	R	R

Drop(flt): shuffle: pu.chge: toe tap: drop(flt): shuffle: pu.chge: toe tap: run.

1	a 2	+	a	3	4	a 5	+	a	6	7

154 Maxi-ford with step – without pick-up (or maxi-ford change) (M/F.w.step) (M/F.chge)

The same as the maxi-ford with a toe tap, but replace the toe tap with a step behind (thus changing weight and changing sides). This type of maxi-ford has the feeling of waltz clog. The counts are the same as the maxi-ford with toe tap. The drop, as before, is on the whole foot.

R(toRS)	L	L(toL)	R(XbL)	L(toLS)	R(toR)	R	L(XbR)	R	L

Drop(flt): (sd)shuffle: spring: step: drop(flt): (sd)shuffle: spring: step: run: run:

<u>1</u>	+ 2	+	3	<u>4</u>	+ 5	+	6	7	8

R	L	L(toL)	R(XbL)	L	R	R(toR)	L(XbR)	R
Drop(flt):	(sd)shuffle:	spring:	step:	drop(flt):	(sd)shuffle:	spring:	step:	run.
1	+ 2	+	3	4	+ 5	+	6	7

Or with a pick-up change

R(toRS)	L	R to L	R(XbL)	L(toLS)	R	L to R	L(XbR)	R	L
Drop(flt):	(sd)shuffle:	pu.chge:	step:	drop(flt):	(sd)shuffle:	pu.chge:	step:	run:	run:
1	a 2	+	a 3	4	a 5	+	a 6	7	8

R(toRS)	L	R to L	R(XbL)	L	R	L to R	L(XbR)	R
Drop(flt):	(sd)shuffle:	pu.chge:	step:	drop(flt):	shuffle:	pu.chge:	step:	run.
1	a 2	+	a 3	4	a 5	+	a 6	7

155 Combination maxi-ford

L	R	R(bL)	L	R	LtoR	L
Spring:	(sd)shuffle:	drop(w.LF under knee):	tap spring:	(b)shuffle:	pu.chge:	toe tap:
8	+ a	1	+ 2	+ 3	+ a	4

L	R	L to R	L
Drop(flt):	(b)shuffle:	pu.chge:	toe tap: (M/F(w.toe tap)
5	a 6	+ a	7

Repeat twice on same foot   8+a1+2+3+a4 5a6+a7 8+a1+2+3+a4 5 a6+a7

Break
(The first step in the break is a hop on the whole foot, and the sound is the same as that of a stamp, scuff or flat drop.)

R	L	R	LtoR	L	L	R	LtoR	L	L
Hop(flt):	drop(flt):	(b)shuffle:	pu.chge:	toe tap:	drop(flt):	(b)shuffle:	pu.chge:	toe tap:	spring.
8	1	a2	+ a	3	4	a 5	+ a	6	7

156 Maxi-ford turn

R	L	LtoR	R	L
Drop(flt):	shuffle:	pu.chge:	step:	step: (making a complete turn to R). Repeat ad lib
1	a 2	& a	3	4

CUTAWAYS

157

R(bL)	L	R(L bent in front)	L(XfR)	R (pass LbR)	L(bR)
Toe tap:	hop:	drop:	toe tap:	hop:	toe tap:
1	+	2	+	3	+

158

R(XfL):	L(passRbk):	R(bL):	R (LXfR):	R(XfL)	L(passRbk)	L(bR)
Toe tap:	hop:	toe tap:	drop:	toe tap:	hop:	toe tap
1	+	2	+	3	+	4

159

L	R(XfL)	L(RL released behind)				
Spring:	toe tap:	hop on whole foot:		repeat commencing RF		
1	+	2		3 + 4		

R(L released behind)	L	R(bL)	R	L(XfR)	R	L(bR)
Hop on whole foot:	spring:	toe tap:	drop:	toe tap:	hop:	toe tap
5	+	6	+	7	+	8

160 Trenches

These steps are like long runs on the spot, with the legs extended well behind and the body leaning forwards as a counter-balance. They can be taken with the simple action of sliding the foot and taking the leg straight back; in this version the arms would move forwards and back in opposition. The other 'proper' version is done with a sliding action on the outside of the foot, making a slight arc shape which continues off the floor so that the foot finishes (as in the simple version) directly behind the body; in this version the arms swing from side to side.

161 Over the top

Another way to describe this step is 'jumping over the foot'. It requires good strength in the torso and thighs. The movement consists of holding the right leg across in front of the left leg (the right knee is almost stretched). The left leg will then take a hop, with a well lifted leg, so that it passes over the right leg. During the hop, the right foot moves back underneath (either sliding along the ground or just above the ground) to give clearance for the left foot to land in front of the right. The movement could first be practised sitting on a chair to familiarize the body with the movements required. It could then be taken holding on to the barre, or with a teacher holding the student's hands. The 'over-the-top' hop can be taken forward or back. It also works very well combined with a cutaway action.

162 Combination 'over the top'

L	R	LtoR	L	L(RXfL)		w.L	
Drop(flt):	(b)shuffle:	pu.chge:	toe tap:	drop:		'over the top':	repeat commencing RF
1	n n	n a	2	3		4	5nnnna6 7 8

Roy Castle demonstrating 'over the top'.
(1) Preparation ...

(2) ... the hop over, moving the underneath foot back ...

Break

L	R	LtoR	L	L(RXfL)	w.L (taking R bk)
Drop(flt):	(b)shuffle:	pu.chge:	toe tap:	drop:	'over the top':
1	n n	n a	2	3	4

w.L (taking R fwd)	w.L (taking R bk)	R(bL)	L	R	L
(back) 'over the top'	'over the top':	toe tap:	hop:	bll.chge.	
5	6	a	7	a	8

Alternative break

L	R	LtoR	L	L(RXfL)	w.L (taking R bk)	L(half turn R to face bk)
Drop(flt):	(b)shuffle:	pu.chge:	toe tap:	drop:	'over the top':	hop: (leave RL XfL)
1	n n	n a	2	3	4	5

w.L	R	L	R	L
'over the top':	toe tap:	hop:	bll.chge.	
6	+	7	+	8

163 Over the top with cutaway

Use any of the 'cutaway' steps. Substitute 'over the top' for passing the foot forwards or back.

164 Falling off the log

This step can be done with or without the shuffle. It usually travels sideways. The body leans so that the step gives the illusion of being off-balance.

Leaning to the left

L	R	R (L stretched XfR to RS):	L(starting to turn body twds L):
Spring:	(sd)shuffle:	drop:	spring:
8	& a	1	2

(XfL release L behind (twds RS): and leaning fwd twds L):	Repeat ad lib
drop	
3	

(3) ... landing from the hop. (Photographs by Julian Clode)

'Over the Top' and 'Trenches'

These steps were popular after World War I. They were so named because the movements imitated that of the soldiers as they climbed out of the trenches and crawled over the top. 'Over the top' was used as a flash step, and a series of 'trenches' was often the final step of a routine.

165 Buffalo – also known as Shuffle off to Buffalo

The step travels sideways and is often used as an exit step. Single, double or triple.

Commence with the RF under the knee in front of LL.

Single

R	L		L(lifting RF in front under knee)
Spring:	(sd)shuffle:		drop:
1	& a		2

Double

R	L		L(lifting RF in front under knee)
Tap spring:	(sd)shuffle:		drop
a 1	& a		2

Triple

R	L		L(lifting RF in front under knee)
Shuffle step:	(sd)shuffle:		drop:
& a 1	& a		2

166 Suzi-Q

This was a dance craze in 1937. With hands clasped and held extended in front of the body, slide the right foot across in front of the left (slightly turned in). Then while stepping to the left with the left foot, lift the toe of the right foot (slightly turned out and leaving the heel on the floor). It was originally a jitterbug step but eventually tap dancers added tapping steps to the movements.

167 Suzie Q with tapping steps

L	R		R(XfL)		L(w.R toe lifted – slightly turned out)
Hop:	(sd)shuffle:	stamp(w) (slightly turned in):			tap step:
8	&	a	1		a 2

R		R		L(w.R toe lifted – slightly turned out)
pu:	stamp(w)(slightly turned in):			tap step:
a	3			a 4

R	L	R	(using same twisting action as in counts 'a3 a4'
pu stamp(w):	tap step:	pu stamp(w):	
a 5	a 6	a 7	

168 Chicago roll

This uses exactly the same twisting action on the 'stamp pick-up step' as the Suzie Q, and the steps are similar. On count '1' (stamp) the RF turns in. On count '+2' (tap step with the LF) the RF turns out, but the R heel remains on the ground.

R	L	R(turned in):	L(R toe out):	R(tog)	L	R	L	R	L(tog)
Shuffle:	hop:	stamp(w):	tap step:	pu step:	shuffle:	hop:	stamp(w):	tap step:	pu step:
+ 8	+	<u>1</u>	+ 2	+ 3	+ 4	+	<u>5</u>	+ 6	+ 7

Hesitation break

R	L	R	L		R		L		R(tog)

Shuffle: hop: stamp: tap step: *(pause):* pu stamp(w): tap step:*(pause):* pu step.

+ 8 + <u>1</u> + 2 (3) + <u>4</u> + 5 (6) + 7

Alternative break

R	L	R	L	R		L	R		L	R

Shuffle: hop: stamp(w): tap step: pu stamp(w): tap step: pu stamp(w): tap step: pu step.

+ 8 + 1 + 2 + 3 + 4 + 5 + 6 + 7

169 American roll

L	R		L(bR)		L	R	L		R

Hop: (sd)shuffle: drop(w.ft under knee): tap spring: tap step: stamp(w): stamp(n):

8 +a 1 + 2 + 3 + <u>4</u>

R	L	R	L	R	L

pu: hop: step: pu: hop: step: repeat ad lib or mix with other similar steps.

+ 5 + 6 + 7

170 Shim Sham

The opening step of the shim sham shimmy. Try the mnemonic chant 'Can you read, Can you write, Can you smoke your Daddy's pipe'.

	R		L		R	R	L		R

Stamp(n) pu step: stamp(n) pu step: stamp(n) pu bll.chge: stamp(n) pu step: repeat L:

8 + 1 2 + 3 4 + 5 + 6 + 7 8+12+34+5+6+7

Essences (Used in 'Soft-shoe' Dances)

Essences were the traditional steps of the soft-shoe style. The style is elegant and calm, with medium to slow tempo. There are many different essences and traditional soft-shoe 'breaks'. Here are some.

171 Single essence

L(toLS)	R(XfL)	R(f) L(b)	

Tap step: brush: bll.chge: repeat commencing RF

a 1 & a 2 a 3 & a 4

172 Back essence

	L	L(XbR)		R(atRS)		L(in place)	

(bk)brush: step: step (momentarily xfer wgt): step: repeat commencing RF

a 1 a 2 a 3 a 4

173 Virginia essence

	L(toLS)		R		L	

Brush step: (fwd)brush heel dig(w.wgt): step (in place): repeat RF

a 1 & a 2 & 3 & a 4

174 Double essence

In this step the working leg moves across the supporting leg; to an open line; then across again.

L(toL)	R (XfL):	L(in place)	R(toR):	L(in place):	R (XfL):	L(in place)
Brush step:	brush step:	step:	brush step:	step:	brush step:	step:
a 1	& a	2	& a	3	& a	4

175 Soft-shoe break

L	R	R	L	R	L	R	R	L	R
Step:	brush(fwd):	heel dig(w):	step:	shuffle:	hop:	(sd)shuffle:	spring:	(sd)shuffle:	hop:
a	1	&	a	2 &	a	3 &	a	4 &	a

L(XfR)	(wgt.on both)	R	L
step:	Twist turn:	stamp(w):	stamp(w):
5	- -	a	8

176 Another break

L	R	R	L	R	L	R	R	L	R
Step:	brush(fwd):	heel dig(w):	step:	shuffle:	hop:	(sd)shuffle:	spring:	(sd)shuffle:	hop:
a	1	&	a	2 &	a	3 &	a	4 &	a

L(XfR)	RF (to RCF)	L(lean slightly bk)	R	L	L	R
step:	scuff(flt):	heelbt:	(bk)brush	step:	pu:	bll.chge
5	a	6	a	7	&	a 8

177 Alternative break

L	R	L	R	L	R(XfL)	L	R	L(fwd)
Tap step:	tap step:	step:	shuffle:	hop:	(sd)shuffle	step:	(fwd)brush:	hop: step:
a 1	& a	2	& a	3	& a	4	&	a 5

R(turn L to face LS)	L(turn L to face front)	R	L
step:	step:	(fwd)brush:	hop
6	7	a	8

178 Another alternative break

L	R	L	R	L	R	L	R(fwd):	L	R
Tap step:	tap step:	step:	(str)shuffle:	hop:	(sd)shuffle:	hop:	step:	brush:	hop:
a 1	& a	2	& a	3	n &	a	4	&	a

L(fwd)	R(fwd to LS)	L	R	L
step:	step($\frac{1}{4}$ turn L):	step (fwd to front w. $\frac{3}{4}$ turn L):	brush:	hop(releasing foot fwd):
5	6	7	a	8

Alternative end:

R	L	R
Chug	chug	chug (releasing the foot forward on the last chug)
&	a	8

Other Soft-Shoe Steps

Grapevine steps and various combinations including toe-heel clips are also used in soft-shoe dances. An example of each is given below.

179 Grapevine step

L	R	R(toRS)	L(XbR)	R	L	L(toLS)	R(XbL)
Hop:	(sd)shuffle:	spring:	touch:	hop:	(sd)shuffle:	spring:	touch:
a	1 &	a	2	a	3 &	a	4

Break (with grapevine)

L	R	R(toRS)	L(XbR)	R(toRS)	L(XfR)	R(toRS)	L(XbR)
Hop:	(sd)shuffle:	spring:	step:	spring:	step:	spring:	step:
a	5 &	a	6	a	7	a	8

180 Toe-heel clip combination

L	R	L	R(XfL)		LtoR	R	L(toLS)
Step:	(sd) shuffle:	heelbt:	step:		toe-heel-clip:	heelbt:	step:
1	a 2	a	3		&	a	4

R	L	L	R		L	L R	L
pu step:	shuffle bll.chge(flt):		shuffle bll.chge:				stamp:
& a	5 & a		6			a 7 & a	8

Time-Steps

Shuffle Time-Steps (also known as Buck Time-Step)

181 Single (shuffle) time-step (sngl t/s)

R	L	R		L	R	
Shuffle:	hop:	step:	(fwd) tap step:	step:		repeat
8 +	1	2	+ 3	+	4 + 5	6 + 7 +

182 Single break (sngl brk)

R	L	R	L		R		L		R
Shuffle:	hop:	step:	shuffle step:		shuffle step:		shuffle step:		stamp (or step):
8 +	1	2	+ 3	+	4 +	5	+ 6	+	7

183 Double (shuffle) time-step (dbl.t/s)

R	L	R		L	R	
Shuffle:	hop:	(fwd)tap step:		(fwd)tap step:	step:	Repeat
8 +	1	+ 2		+ 3	+	4 + 5 + 6 + 7 +

184 Double break (dbl.brk)

R	L	R	L		R		L	R
Shuffle:	hop:	tap step:	shuffle step:		shuffle step:		shuffle step:	stamp(w):
8 +	1	+ 2	+ 3	+	4 +	5	+ 6	+ 7

185 Triple (shuffle) time-step (trpl.t/s)

R	L	R		L	R					
Shuffle:	hop:	(sd)shuffle step:		(f)tap step:	step:		repeat			
8 +	1	+ a	2	+	3	+	4 + 5 + a 6 + 7 +			

186 Triple break (trpl.brk)

R	L	R	L	R	L	R
Shuffle:	hop:	(sd)shuffle step:	shuffle step:	shuffle step:	shuffle step:	stamp:
8 +	1	+ a 2	+ 3	+ 4	+ 5	+ 6	+ 7

Off-Beat and Pick-Up Time Steps

187 Off-beat time step (also known as buck, negro or old time-step)

Facing front

R	L	R	L	R
Stamp(n):	hop:	spring:	tap step:	stamp(w):	repeat commencing LF
8	1	2	+ 3	+	4 5 6 + 7 +

Pick-Up Time-Steps (pu.t/s)

(also called Off-Beat, Buck, Negro or Old Time-Step)

This time-step is the same as the off-beat time-step described above, but a back brush or pick-up is added immediately after the first stamp each time. These can also be taken facing the diagonals. The first stamp(n) with the RF would face LCF, and then use alternate diagonals for each successive time-step.
(The use of even eighths or eighth-note triplets in the rhythm will depend on the music used.)

188 Single pick-up time-step (pu.sngl.t/s)

Commence facing RCF with RF flat and slightly forward

R	R	L	R	L	R
Stamp(n):	pu:	hop:	spring:	tap step:	stamp(w):	repeat commencing LF
8	+	1	2	+ 3	+	4 + 5 6 + 7 + 8

Break

R	R	L	R	L	R	L(RXFL)	R	L	R
Stamp(n):	pu:	hop:	spring:	shuffle step:	shuffle:	hop:	tap step:	bll.chge:
8	+	1	2	+ 3	+	4 +	5	+ 6	+ 7

189 Double pick-up time-step (pu.dbl.t/s) and break

As for single, but substitute tap spring (+2) instead of spring (2)

190 Triple pick-up time-step (pu.trpl.t/s) and break

As for single, but substitute shuffle step (+a2) instead of spring (2)

Cramp Roll (or Roll) Time-Steps

191 Single

R	L	R	L	R	L
pu:	hop:	spring:	tap step:	step heelbt:	stamp(n):
a	1	2	a 3	& a	4

192 Double

As for single, but substitute tap spring (&2) instead of spring (2): i.e. a1 a2 a3&a4

193 Triple

As for single, but substitute (sd)shuffle step (&a2) instead of spring (2): i.e. a1&a2&a3&a4

194 Double triple

As for triple, but substitute (sd)shuffle step (&a3) instead of tap step (a3): i.e.a1&a2&a3&a4

195 Double triple with 4s.cramp roll (or double triple with drum)

As for double triple, but insert a 4s. cramp roll.

```
R   L     R                L      L
pu: hop: (sd)shuffle step: (sd)shuffle 4s.crmp.rl: stamp(n):
a   1     &a    2          &a       3nna    4
```

NOTE: In the time-step a heelbt could be used instead of the stamp(n) on the count of '4'.

Travelling Time-Steps (also known as Cubanola)

196 Single (basic)

(travel sideways to R)

```
   R            L    L R   L R   R    L        R
(sd)shuffle step:  (sd)shuffle: bll.chge: bll.chge: hop:  spring:  shuffle step:  repeat L
   8 +    1       + 2   + 3   + 4    5    6      + 7  +
```

197 Double (basic)

(travel sideways to R)

```
   R            L    L R   L R   R    L        R
(sd)shuffle step: (sd)shuffle: bll.chge: bll.chge: hop: tap spring: shuffle step:  repeat L
   8 +    1       + 2   + 3   + 4    5    + 6      + 7  +
```

198 Triple (basic)

(travel sideways to R)

```
   R            L    L R   L R   R        L     R
(sd)shuffle step:  (sd)shuffle: bll.chge: bll.chge: hop:  shuffle step: shuffle step:  repeatL
   8 +    1       + 2   + 3   + 4    5    & a   6   +7  +
```

199 Break

There are various breaks for the travelling time-step. One version is as follows:

```
L     R     L     R     L R     L R     L R
Shuffle step: shuffle: hop: (sd)shuffle: hop:  toe tap: hop: tap step: bll.chge
  8 + 1   + 2   +       3 + 4    + 5   + 6   +  7
```
(Travel to RCF on '+ 6 + 7')

200 Travelling time-step adding a pick-up

Each of the single, double and triple time-steps above can be taken with a pick-up immediately before the hop – making the count + 5 each time. The break is the same as above.

FAKE WING TIME-STEP OR MOCK WING TIME-STEP

(*also known as* Preparation Wing Time-Step)

Fake Wing Time-Step Taking One Bar of Music

(*Note:* On the count of '3', the 'step' of the tap step is executed simultaneously with the 'slide' at the beginning of the fake wing. This applies to the one-bar and the two-bar fake wing time-steps).

201 Single fake wing time-step (one bar)

Commence facing front with RF in front of LF

R	L	R	L	R	L		
pu:	hop:	spring:	tap step:	(fk)wing:	stamp(n):	repeat LF:	repeat RF:
a	1	2	a 3	& a 4		a5 6 a7&a8	a1 2a3&a4

Break

R	L	R	L	R	L	R
pu:	hop:	spring:	shuffle:	hop:	step:	stamp(n):
a	5	6	& a	7	a	8

202 Double fake wing time-step (one bar)

As for the single, but execute a tap spring (a2) instead of a spring (2)
Break
   Substitute 'tap spring' on the count of (&2)

203 Triple fake wing time-step (one bar)

As for the single, but execute a side shuffle step (&a2) instead of a spring (2)
Break
   Substitute a 'shuffle step' on the counts of (&a2)

204 Double-Triple fake wing time-step (one bar)

As for the triple, but substitute a side shuffle step (&a3) for the tap step (+3)
Break
   Substitute a 'shuffle step' on the counts of (&a2) and on (&a3)

Fake Wing Time-Steps Using Two Bars of Music
205 Single fake wing time-step (two bars)

Commence facing front with RF in front of LF

R	L	R	L(tog)	R	L(XR)	R(b)	L	R (XbL)	L	R
pu:	hop:	spring:	tap step:	(fk)wing:	shuffle step:	shuffle:	pu1ft:	shuffle step:	step:	stamp(n):
a	1	2	a 3	&a 4	& a 5	& a 6	& a 7	a 8		

   Dance the time-step three times

Fake or Mock Wing Time-Steps Using Two Bars of Music

On counts 3&a4&a5&a6&a7 the rhythm should be absolutely even. This is a difficult rhythm to control and maintain. It is helpful if the landing from the pick-up on one foot is delayed. To achieve this feeling of suspension, straighten the 'underneath' leg and breathe in during the elevated part of the pick-up on one foot.

Break
There are many breaks. The following is one example:

Lift the RF behind

L	R	L	R	L	R	L	R	L	R	L	R	L
Hop:	flap:	tap spring:	tap spring:	tap spring:	toe tap:	hop:	spring:	toe tap:	hop:	step:	step:	stamp(n)
n	na1	a 2	a 3	a 4	a	5	a	6	a	7	a	8

206 Double fake wing time-step (two bars)
The same as the single fake wing time-step (two bars), but substitute 'tap spring' on the count 'a2'.

207 Triple fake wing time-step (two bars)
The same as the single fake wing time-step (two bars), but substitute '(sd)shuffle step' at count '&a2'.

208 Double-Triple fake wing time-step (two bars)
The same as the triple fake wing time-step (two bars), but substitute another '(sd)shuffle step' at count '&a3'.

Time-Steps Combining Fake Wings and Real Wings

209 One-bar fake wing time-step combined with single wing
One-bar fake wing time-step commencing RF (201), but transfer weight on the last stamp

a1 2 a3&a4

R	R	L	R	L
Drop:	3s.sngl wing:	bll.chge:	stamp(n):	repeat commencing LF: repeat RF: break as for two bar t/s.
5	na6	a 7	8	a1 – 8

210 Two-bar fake wing time-step combined with single wing
Fake wing time-step to two bars commencing RF (No. 205), but transfer weight on the last stamp.
a1 2a3&a4&a5&a6&a7 a8

R	L R	R	L R	R	L R	L
3s.sngl wing:	bll.chge:	3s.sngl wing:	bll.chge:	3s.sngl wing:	bll.chge:	stamp(n):
na1	a 2	na3	a 4	na5	a 6	7

Develop this time-step by using the double time-step in the fake-wing sections, and 4s.wing or 5s.wing in the real-wing sections.

211 Wings or fake wings 4s.
(This exercise uses a 4s.sngl wing with the heelbt on the sup. foot to make the fourth sound)

R   L   R   L   R
pu: hop: tap step: tap step (w.overlap) into 4s. fk. wing (single wing with heelbt)
a   1   a   2   a   3   nna4

 L   R   R   L   R
Tap step (w.overlap) into 4s. fk wing: lift LF: 4s.wing with heelbt: step: stamp(n):
 a   5   nna6   nna7   a   8

R   L   R   L   R   R   L   R L   L
pu: hop: tap step: tap step into 4s. fk. wing: lift LF: 4s.wing: shuffle: bll.chge: stamp(n):
a   1   a   2   a   3   nna4   nna5   a 6   & a   7

212 Supported wing time-step
This sequence uses a variation of the toe-tap time-step (No. 229) combined with a fake wing, which is supported from a toe beat behind the working leg.

   R   L   R   L(fwd)   R
Shuffle: hop: toe tap step: tap-step heelbt: toe beat (leave RF on the ground)
 1 +   2   + 3   + 4   +   5

L (supported by R) L (supported by R)   R
  3s.single wing: 3s.single wing: stamp(w):
     na6   na7   8

Repeat LF   repeat RF

Break
   L   R   L   R   L   R
Shuffle: hop: tap step heelbt: *(miss):* tap step heel: *(miss):* chug: chug: *(miss):*
 1 +   2   + 3   ±   *(4)*   + 5   ±   *(6)*   +   7   *(8)*

Try the same time-step with a real wing by using a toe tap instead of a toe beat on count 5.

(Real) Wing Time-Steps
213 Single-wing time-step
   R   L   L   R(bL)   L   R   L   R   L
Shuffle: hop: 3s.sngl wing: (sd)shuffle step: shuffle: hop: shuffle step: tap step: step.
 8 +   1   na2   e +   3   4 +   5   e +   6   + 7   +

Repeat twice with the same foot 8+1 na2e+ 3 4+5e+ 6+7+ 8+1 na2e+ 3 4+5e+6+ 7+

Break
   R   L   R   L   R(XfL)   L   R
Shuffle: hop: (sd)shuffle step: (str)shuffle step: (str) shuffle: hop: 4s.riff.
 8 +   1   e +   2   + 3   +   4 +   5   + 6 + 7

98

(The use of the count 'e +' for some of the shuffles is deliberate. The rhythm on these particular shuffles is clipped, with a very small space between the '+' and the following count, i.e. sufficient for (a) to represent the slight pause.)

214 Change-wing time-step

R	L	L to R	L	R	
Shuffle:	hop:	chge wing:	tap step:	step:	repeat L
8 +	1	na2	+ 3	+	4+5+a6+7+

Break

R	L	L to R	R	R to L	L to R	L	L R
Shuffle:	hop:	chge wing:	hop:	chge wing:	chge wing:	shuffle	bll.chge(flt)
8 +	1	na2	3	na4	na5	+ 6	+ 7

Scuff Time-Steps (Using the Flat Scuff)

215 Scuff time-step – single

R	L	R(bL)	L(toLS)	R	
Scuff:	hop:	step:	tap step:	stamp(w):	repeat LF
1	2	3	+ 4	+	5 6 7+8+

Break

R	L	R(bL)	L	R	L	R L	R	
Scuff:	hop:	step:	pu step:	tap step:	tap step:	bll.chge:	flap:	(trav. fwd)
1	2	3	+ 4	+ 5	+ 6	+ 7	n8	

216 Scuff time-step – double

R	L	R(bL)	L	R	
Scuff:	hop:	(bk)tap step:	tap step:	stamp(w):	repeat LF
1	2	+ 3	+ 4	+	5 6 + 7 + 8 +

Break – double

R	L	R(bL)	L	R	L	R L	R	
Scuff:	hop:	(bk)tap step:	pu step:	tap step:	tap step:	bll.chge:	flap:	(trav.fwd)
1	2	+ 3	+ 4	+ 5	+ 6	+ 7	n8	

217 Scuff time-step – triple

R	L	R (bL)	L(toLS)	R	
Scuff:	hop:	(sd)shuffle step:	tap step:	stamp(w):	repeat LF
1	2	+ a 3	+ 4	+	5 6 +a7 + 8 +

Break – triple

R	L	R(bL)	L	R	L	R L	R	
Scuff:	hop:	(sd)shuffle step:	pu step:	tap step:	tap step:	bll.chge:	flap:	(trav.fwd)
1	2	+ a 3	+ 4	+ 5	+ 6	+ 7	n8	

218 Stamp-scuff time-step – single   (Not corrected because of box in the way)

(Commence facing front)

R	R	R	L	R(XbL)	L(toLS)	R	L	R(Xf)
Stamp(n):	stamp(n):	scuff:	hop:	step:	step:	shuffle:	hop:	step:
1	2	3	4	5	6	+ 7	+	8

Repeat L
1 2 3 4 5 6+7+8

Repeat R
1 2 3 4 5 6+7+8

Break – single

L	R	L	R(XbL)	L	L R	L R
Stamp(w):	scuff:	hop:	step:	shuffle:	bll.chge:	bll.chge:
1	2	3	4	+ 5	+ 6	+ 7

219 Stamp-scuff time-step – double

As for single, but substitute '(bk)tap step' at count '+5'

Break – double

As for single, but substitute '(bk)tap step' at count '+4'.

220 Stamp-scuff time-step – triple

As for single, but substitute '(sd)shuffle step' at count '+a5'

Break – triple

As for single, but substitute '(sd)shuffle step' at count '+a4'

> ### Stamp Scuff Time-Step
>
> Add style to the stamp scuff time-step by circling the working leg outwards after the scuff. While doing so, also turn slightly towards the right so that the body moves with the leg and simulates the shape of a 'figure 8'. Lean away from the working leg. Develop the step further by taking 'tap step (+6)' instead of 'step (6)' in each of the time steps.

221 Travelling stamp scuff time-step

R	L	R(circleLout)	L	R	L	L R	L R
Stamp:	scuff:	stomp:	(bk)brush step:	pu step:	shuffle	bll.chge(flt):	bll.chge(flt):
1	2	3	+ 4	+ 5	+ 6	+ 7	+ 8

L R	L	R(circleLout)	L	R	L	L R	
Bll.chge(flt):	scuff:	stomp:	(bk)brush step:	pu step:	shuffle	bll.chge(flt):	*(miss):*
+ 1	2	3	+ 4	+ 5	+ 6	+ 7	*(8)*

L(to LS)	R(XfL)	L	L(XfR)	L(XfR)
Tap step heelbt:	tap step heelbt:	(fwd)brush:	(bk)brush:	step heelbt:
+ 1	2 + 3	4	5	6 7 8

R	L R	L	R	L R	L
Stamp:	scuff: stomp:	(bk)brush step:	pu step:	shuffle heelbt:	toe-tap: (miss):
1	2 3	+ 4	+ 5	+ 6 +	7 (8)

Riff Time-Steps

Note: Use the following time-step to practise getting even sounds within the spaces between the beats. The use of the different signs for the 'and' is deliberate. The counts +1+2+3+4 are meant to be even. The use of '&a1&a2' represents the even spacing of the three sounds between the beat, whereas '+a1' represents a part of 'e+a1' (16th notes).

In the following riff time-step sequence the first one (no. 222) is confined to even eighth notes. The remainder produce a gradual build-up of the use of controlling triplet rhythm across even music. (Music suggestion – use Bosanova or Beguine.)

222 Four-sound riff time-step (4s.riff.t.s)

	R		L		R					

Shuffle: heelbt: 4s.riff: repeat commencing LF:
8 +   1   + 2 + 3 4 + 5 + 6 + 7

Break

		R			L	R		L			R	

Shuffle step heelbt: heelbt: 4s.riff: tap step heelbt: tap step heelbt:
8 + 1   +   2   +3+4 + 5   +   6 +   7

223 Five-sound riff time-step (5s.riff.t.s)

	R		L		R	

Shuffle: heelbt L: 5s.riff: repeat commencing LF
8 +   1   &a2+3 4+5+a6+7

Break

	R			L	R		L			R

Shuffle step heelbt: heelbt: 5s.riff: tap step heelbt: tap step heelbt:
8 + 1   +   2   &a3a4 + 5   + 6 +   7

224 Six-sound riff time-step (6s.riff.t.s)

	R		L		R	

Shuffle: heelbt: 6s.riff: repeat commencing LF
8 +   1 &a2&a3 4+5&a6&a7

Break

	R			L	R		L			R

Shuffle step heelbt: heelbt: 6s.riff: tap step heelbt: tap step heelbt:
8 + 1   +   2   &a3&a4 + 5   + 6 +   7

225 Seven-sound riff time-step (7s.riff.t.s)

	R		L		R	

Shuffle: heelbt: 7s.riff: repeat commencing LF
8   +   1 &a2e+a3 4+5+a6e+a7

Break

	R(bk)			L	R		L			R

Shuffle: step: heelbt: heelbt: 7s.riff: tap step heelbt: tap step heelbt
8 + 1   +   2   &a3e+a4   + 5 + 6 +   7

Other Time-Steps
226 Open or Astaire time-step

	R	L	R(op.diag.b)		L	LXR	R			
Shuffle:	hop:	step:		pu:	bll.	chge:	repeat L:		repeat R:	
8 +	1	2		+	3	+	4+5 6+7+		8+1 2+3+	

Break

	L	R(fwd)	R(XfL)		L		R	
Shuffle:	step:	shuffle:		spring:	toe tap:			
4 +	5	+ 6		+	7			

227 Manhattan time-step (also known as 'Hoofer time-step')

	R	L	R	L	R		L		R
Stamp(w):	stamp(w):	stamp(w):	stamp(w):	pu step:	stamp(n)	pu step:	stamp(w):		
a	8	a	1	a 2	a	3 a	4		

	L	R	L
Tap step:	tap step:	shuffle:	
a 5	a 6	a 7	

228 Variation on Manhattan time-step

Commence with RF slightly behind LF. The first three chugs change weight but the fourth one does not. At the end of the phrase leave the RF on the floor ready for repeat on same foot.

	L	R	L	R		L		R	L	R
Chug:	chug:	chug:	chug pu step:	stamp(n)	pu step:	stamp(n)	pu step:	tap step:	tap step:	
a	8	a	1 a 2	a	3 a	4	a 5	a 6	a 7	

The above can also be taken with six instead of four chugs at the beginning – counted as follows:

	L	R	L	R	L	R		L		R
Chug:	chug:	chug:	chug:	chug:	chug pu step:	stamp(n)	pu step:	stamp(n)	pu step:	
&	a 8	&	a	1 a 2	a	3 a	4	a 5		

	L	R
tap step:	tap step:	repeat same foot
a 6	a 7	

229 Toe-tap time-step

	R	L	R	L	R	
Shuffle:	hop:	toe tap step:	tap step:	step:	repeat commencing LF	
8 +	1	+ 2	+ 3	+	4+5+6+7+	

Break

	R	L	R	L	R	L	L R
Shuffle:	hop:	toe tap step:	shuffle step:	shuffle step:	shuffle bll.chge.		
8 +	1	+ 2	+ 3	+ 4 +	5	+ 6	+ 7

7 CLASS PLAN AND EXERCISES

PLANNING CLASSES

Enthusiastic beginners are always anxious to achieve clever rhythmic sounds immediately. However, progress will be quicker if they first master the steps of 'one sound'. 'Two sounds' should follow, with the gradual introduction of the remainder. For those following an examination syllabus there is a required order for teaching the steps. Various options are open to teachers devising their own programme; the following is a suggestion.

Example of Class Structure
* Warm-up
* Introducing new steps
* Rhythm and timing
* Simple exercises
* Time-steps
* Traditional steps
* Exercises for line and style, turning and ground pattern
* Close work
* Improvisation
* Sequences

Preparation
Preparation prior to class should include some form of simple, limbering warm-up. Exercises from jazz or modern dance are suitable, for example gentle reaches, shoulder shrugging, circling and relaxing; stretching out the backs of the legs, and some slow rises.

Warm-Up
The aim of the technical warm-up is to relax the knees, ankles and feet. Shuffles combined with shaking of the leg (completely relaxing the foot) are ideal, as are knee flexions, jumps, springs, hops, tap springs and tap-step ball changes. Simple, easily remembered arrangements are essential. Memorizing complex sequences often causes tension, thus defeating the object.

Introducing New Steps
Take these in a series in place, travelling forwards or backwards, in lines or on diagonals. Correct leg and foot action should be the first consideration. Clarity of tone is the eventual aim, and later the development of the finer qualities of light and shade, use of accent, and variation in level of tone to make the rhythms 'rhythmical'.

Rhythm Patterns
New rhythm patterns should be introduced at each level. Initially adhere to a simple basic rhythm to concentrate on keeping time: start with quarter notes to teach time-keeping. Next, devise simple rhythm patterns to include eighth notes (even eighths and eighth-note triplets). Simple use of syncopation – as an integral part of tap dancing – should be included at an early stage. At successive levels introduce twelfth notes, sixteenth notes, twentieths (and more); also 'clusters' of sound, doubling the time, crossing the phrase, various musical rhythm patterns and different time signatures. Clapping or counting a given rhythm often aids understanding.

Simple Exercises
Arrange short sequences encompassing newly learned technical steps (as many or as few as the participants can assimilate in the time available).

Allow time at every lesson to listen to each pupil separately. Faulty rhythm is easier to correct in the early stages of learning. Listen without watching occasionally (by just turning the head away); this sharpens the sense of hearing. Students should also be encouraged to listen to themselves.

Starting with the simplest of each type, traditional steps and time-steps can be phased in whenever considered relevant.

Line and Style, Ground Pattern, Turning Steps

Good posture and good eye-line are essential ingredients for line and style and for turns. Breadth of line, easy co-ordinated movements and a sense of performance enhance style. Arranged sequences can be enhanced with the conscious use of ground pattern (using all available space) and possibly use of levels.

To develop the ability to turn, there are some steps more suitable than others, for instance, step heelbt; tap-step heelbt: tap-step ball change: pick-up ball change: waltz clog: half breaks from the shuffle time-steps: rattles.

In close work, use short sequences to develop quick, small footwork.

Improvisation

Various methods are popular, and a format should be established before commencement. Circle formation is one of the traditional methods, when everyone dances the first four bars of the shim sham and each dancer then improvises separately, the shim sham being danced *ensemble* between each soloist. Line formation could also be used, and dancers either demonstrate together or individually in turn, or are chosen at random.

The method of improvisation could be varied, and the following are a few ideas:

1. Clap (or count) and dance a given rhythm (individually or together).
2. Improvise freely, with no restrictions on rhythm or steps (individually).
3. Specific steps are chosen, but others can be included.
4. Specific steps are stipulated and no others are allowed.

5. Each dancer must start with the last step used by the previous dancer.
6. Each soloist dances and then sets the rhythm for the next dancer.
7. Dancers respond spontaneously to a given rhythm.
8. Dance the shim sham to commence only. Then each dancer improvises separately, each stating (by a show of fingers) how many bars they intend to dance. Successive dancers must be ready for their turn.
9. Spontaneous imitation of series of rhythms, in question-and-answer formation. One or two bars of rhythm clapped or given verbally by the teacher. (There is an excellent track of music for this type of improvisation on the CD *Gone Tappin'*, track 10, *Minor Yours*.)
10. The ultimate aim in improvisation is for the rhythm of the tap dancer to become an integral part of the overall sound. This is true whether improvising or performing a prepared routine. To develop such spontaneous ability, a different piece of music should be chosen each week; the dancers should listen several times and then, individually, attempt an improvisation that will blend with the musical composition. (CD number 2 has a track with a variation in time signature, and numbers 25 and 27 have tracks where the variation in tempo and mood makes them ideal for this exercise.)

Another traditional (and exciting) method of improvisation is the 'hoofers' circle': in this, the hoofers all dance continuous paddle and roll, and shout as they do so; then each takes a turn to show clever or flash steps.

Dance Sequences

Based on technique, rhythm, style and presentation of the relevant level, these could be changed every week, or the same sequence developed for several weeks. The value of the latter is that the dancer learns the art of perfecting a routine for a performance.

Based on the foregoing criteria, the following plan for introducing new vocabulary is divided into ten phases; it can be modified to accommodate individual needs. For amusement the ten elements, starting at absolute beginner, have been given alphabet, as well as numerical levels. Phase 0 is 'Z', representing 'zero knowledge'; from Z, a big jump to 'H' for 'hopeful', to G for 'gaining', F for 'further' and E for 'excellent' knowledge. At the top end there is D for 'dextrous', C for 'clever', B for 'better' or 'best', A for 'ace'. Finally AA represents 'A...a...amazing tapper'.

The example for class structure, together with the suggested phase content, can be used as a basis for devising a series of lessons. Any of the ideas for exercises and sequences can be included where considered relevant.

Phase Z (0)
Rhythm: ¼ notes and 8th note triplets (accented 8th notes).
Vocabulary: *One-sound* steps (selected) only. (str)tap (1): (fwd)tap(3): (fwd)brush(4): (bk)tap(5): (bk)brush(6): pu(7): heel tap(8): ball tap(9): toe tap(10): ball beat(11): heelbt(12): toe beat(13): ball dig(16): touch(17): heel dig(18): hop(19): jump(20): spring(21): step(24): stamp(w)(26). (Exclude 2, 14, 15, 22, 23, 27, 28, 29, 30, 31, 32, 33 to 38.)
Improvisation: Line formation. Clap and dance ¼ notes and 8th note triplets (accented 8th notes). Skips or sideways gallops are suitable for the 8th notes.

Phase H (1)
Rhythm: As in phase Z, plus even 8th notes.
Vocabulary: *One sound*: stamp(n)(27): scuff(hl)(32); *two sounds*: (str)shuffle(40): flap(45): tap step(46): tap spring(47): bll.chge(48): step-heelbt(49): heel ball(50): pu step(51); *three sounds*: tap-step-heel(59): tap-heel-ball(60); *four sounds*: tap-step bll.chge(69): shuffle hop step(70).
Improvisation: As the previous level, with the addition of even 8th notes.

Phase G (2)
Rhythm: As in previous levels, plus 12th notes and missing beats. (Include subtle syncopation in the sequences, but not in the analysis.)
Vocabulary: *One sound*: drop(bll)(22): drop(flt)(23): stomp(28): chug(29): slam(30): scuff(flt)(31): *two sounds*: (sd)shuffle(41); *three sounds*: pu hop step(61): pu spring step(62).
Time-steps: Off-beat time-step(187).
Improvisation: Line formation. As in previous levels, plus 12th notes and missed beats.

Phase F (3)
Rhythm: As in previous levels. Mix the note values used previously.
Vocabulary: bk.shuffle(42): pu.chge(52): pu bll.chge(63): shuffle spring(64): 2s.open.riff.fwd (72): 4s.cramp-roll(88). (Use rhythm a1 a2 initially. Progress to 'cluster' sound at a higher level.)
Time-steps: Shuffle time-step (181): and break (182): scuff time-step (215): simple close work.
Improvisation: Line formation. Clap and dance to a mixed rhythm.

Phase E (4)
Rhythm: As in previous levels, plus 16th notes and syncopation. (Use clusters in the sequences, but not in the analysis.)
Vocabulary: *One sound*: prog.tap(2): toe-beat drag (14); *two sounds*: shuffle(Xf)(44): clip-bll.chge(65): 2s.open.riff.bk(73); *other steps*: 3s.open.riff.fwd(74): 3s.open.riff.bk(75): 4s.riff(76): 5s.cramp-roll(89): pull-back(98): single waltz(sdwys)(107): Bambalina(133).
Traditional steps: Shim sham(170).
Time-steps: Shuffle time-steps(183): pu.t/s sngl(188). Riff t/s(222). Close work.
Improvisation: Mixed rhythm up to 16th notes to include syncopation and/or missed beats – two-bar phrase. Given steps (iii) from class plan. Line or circle formation. With or without shim sham.

Phase D (5)
Rhythm: As previous levels. Plus 20th notes, clusters, and an element of cross-phrasing.
Vocabulary: 2s.hop(57): 2s.spring(58): dbl.shuffle(68): 5s.riff(77): 6s.cramp roll(90): shuffle-pu.chge(102): 3s.ripple(104): 4s.ripple(105): single waltz(r)(108): single waltz(b)(109): double waltz(110): paddle (to front only)(124): cahito(or draw-back)(132).
Time-steps: Triple shuffle t/s(185): break(186): pu double and triple(189), (190). Using tacits.
Traditional steps: M/F with toe tap (153). Close work.
Improvisation: Use (2), (3), (4) from class plan. Circle or line formation. With or without shim sham.

Phase C (6)
Rhythm: Development from earlier levels.
Vocabulary: All remaining *one-sound* steps. Snatch(33): heel clip(34): toe clip(35): toe-heel clip (36): heel-toe clip(37): toe-heel clip.trav.(38): scuffle(55): 3s.shuffle(66): 3s.flap(67): 6s.riff(78): cramp-roll.chge(91): sh.cramp roll.5s.(92): sh. cramp roll.6s.(93): trng.cramp roll(94): trng. cramp-roll.chge.(95): sntch.pull-back(99): paddle (to the side)(124): step-heel(128): sngl.trav.(130): dbl.trav.(131).
Time-steps: Shuffle and pu t/s to include tacit in the music or dance. fake wing t/s(201): scuff t/s (215): riff t/s(222): Astaire t/s(226).
Traditional steps: M/F w. step (154): Close Work. Chicago roll (168): American roll (169).
Improvisation: Anything from previous level, plus (5), (6) and (7) from class plan.

Phase B (7)
Rhythm: All note values including clusters within any time signature. Syncopation, cross-phrasing. Long and short phrases. Tacit. Stop-time.
Vocabulary: Rev.scuffle(56): 8s.riff(80): x.x.riff(81): 5s.hopping riff(82): 6s.hopping riff(83): 7s.hopping riff(84): standing cramp roll(97): opn.&clsd.pull-backs(100): dbl.shuffle.pu.chge.(103): rippledown (106): dbl.paddle(125): paddle.break(126): rattle(134): prog.rattle(135): dbl.toe-tap.rattle(136): dbl.toe-tap.prog.rattle(137).

Time-steps: Mock wing t/s to two bars: cramp roll t/s single, double and triple. Cubanola: Manhattan t/s. Close work.
Traditional steps: M/F turning: essences.
Improvisation: Use (2), (7) and (9) from class plan. Use of various types of music.

Phase A (8)
Rhythm: As in Phase B.
Vocabulary: 6s.hop-heel.riff(85): 7s.hop-heel. riff(86): 8s.hop-heel.riff(87): press cramp roll(96): tip-top pull-back(101): 5s.paddle(127): ball-heel turn(129).
Time-steps: Cramp roll t/s, double-trip with drum: real wing time-steps. Close work.
Traditional steps: Combination M/F: Combination over the top.
Improvisation: All elements in any formation.

Phase A....A (9)
Rhythm: As in previous levels.
Vocabulary: All remaining steps from the vocabulary, time-steps, traditional steps. All sequences from remaining chapters. Ability to create own arrangements.
Improvisation: Use (10) from class work plan, to as many different rhythms and styles as possible.

Customizing the Classes

Refer to the 'Example of Class Structure' when preparing the content of each phase. Include sequences for elevated work as well as for close work. Take account of the age, ability and aim of the pupils; the style and the degree of control will differ between a vocational student and an adult who is simply dancing for recreation. There will also be a difference between the ability of a young beginner and an older child who is already training in other forms of dance. A prop, such as a hat, stick or umbrella, is an asset in a dance if co-ordinated arm lines have not been mastered.

Adult amateur dancers enjoying an opportunity for performance. (Photograph by Keith Walter)

Notes of Exercises

The following examples might be useful as a guide or a catalyst for invention. Short exercises are useful for listening to individual progress. Each sequence has a vocabulary list to establish prerequisite knowledge, suggested tempo and idea for music. The metronome marking represents the dancer's quarter-note count. The counts are given as '+ 1' and 'e+a1' for even 8th notes and 16th notes; and 'a1' and '&a1' for 12th notes and 8th note triplets. Missed counts are noted in brackets in italic *( )*.

230 Vocabulary check: One-sound steps.
    Tempo: Between 138 and 200.
    Music suggestion: CD.15. Track 1 = 156: CD.1 Track 1 = 169: CD.1 Track 8 = 200.

```
                R                    L                   R
(fwd)brush (bk)brush step: (fwd)brush (bk)brush step: step heelbt
     1         2       3        4          5       6     7    8
```
Travel fwd to RCF
```
     L              R(bL)          L                R(bL)        L               R
Heel-dig ball-beat:  step:  heel-dig ball-beat: (miss):  step:  heel-dig ball-beat: stamp(w):
     1         2       3        4          +      (5)      +        6         7        8
```

Travel to RS
```
L(tog)     R(toRS)   L(tog)   R(toRS)          L     R                L(bsdR)
Step:    stamp(w):   step:   stamp(w): (miss) step: stamp(w): (miss) step   heelbt:
  1         2          3        +       (4)    5       +       (6)     +       7
```

```
                R                 L(toLS)  R(bL)    L               L        R(ft tog)
(fwd)brush (bk)brush step:   stamp:   step:  heel-dig (miss) ball-beat: step heelbt: (miss)
     8          1       2        3       4        +      (5)       +       6    7     (8)
```

231 Vocabulary check: One-sound steps.
    Tempo: 120 developing to 132.
    Music suggestion: CD.12 Track 2 = 121.

```
        R              L      R                  L
3 (str)taps step: 1 (str)tap step: step heelbt: 2 straight taps step heelbt: (miss):
1 2 3    4          5   6    7    8    1    2    3    ±    (4)
```

```
R(toL)  R(to side)   L(toR)  L(to side) R(sdwys to RCF)  L(tog)           R(sdwys to RCF)
touch      step:     touch     step:     step heelbt:   ball dig(w): (miss):  step  heelbt:
  5          6         7         8         1     2        ±          (3)      4      +
```

```
L(tog)           R(fwd to RCF)  L(tog)  R(to side)   L (to LS)
Step:  clap: clap:  stamp(w):     clap:    step:    stamp(w):  clap
  5     +     6       ±            7        +          8        +
```

```
       L(to LS)                     L               R
3 prog.taps step heel-tap (miss): heel-tap heelbt: (miss): toe-tap step:
   1   +  2    3      +     (4)      5       +       (6)     +      7
```

232 Vocabulary check: One-sound steps.
    Tempo: Between 120 and 170.
    Music suggestion: CD.1(1) = 169: (6) = 120: (11) = 128.
The sequence starts with a grapevine figure (often used in soft-shoe dances).

Travel sideways to RCF

R(sd)	L(b)	R(sd)	L(f)	R(sd)		L(tog)			R(sd)		L(tog)
Step:	step:	step:	step:	step:	clap:	step:	clap:	clap:	step:	clap:	step:
1	2	3	4	5	+	6	+	7	+	8	+

R(fwd RCF):	L(replace):	R(hlf.trn.to LCB):	L		L			L	R	
Step:	step:	step heelbt:	toe-tap:	clap:	step:	clap:	clap:	heelbt:	heelbt:	clap:
1	2	3 4	5	+	6	+	7	+	8	+

L(toR):	L(sd):	R(to L):	R(sd):	L(toR):		L(sd):			R(toL):		R(sd):	R	L
Touch	step:	touch	step:	touch:	clap:	step:	clap:	clap:	touch:	clap:	step:	heelbt:	heelbt:
1	2	3	4	5	+	6	+	7	+	8	+	1	+

	R		L(fwd)	R(fwd)		L(bk)	R(tog)	L	R	
(miss):	heel-dig	ball-beat:	stamp(w):	stamp(w):	*(miss):*	step:	step:	chug:	chug:	*(miss):*
(2)	+	3	4	+	*(5)*	+	6	7	±	*(8)*

233 Vocabulary check: Building up shuffle hop step.
    Tempo: Approximately 120.
    Music suggestion: CD.16(13): CD.15(14): CD.1(3)(6): CD.6(1)(4): CD.14a(8).

Using straight shuffle. Moving backwards.

R		L	R(bk)	L(bk)	R		L	R(bk)	L(bk)	R		L	R(bk)	L		R	L
Shuffle:	hop:	step:	step:	shuffle:	hop:	step:	step:	shuffle:	hop:	step:	shuffle:	hop:	step:				
a	1	a	2	3	a 4	a	5	6	a 7	a	8	a 1	a	2			

R L	R		L R L R	L		R	L R	L		R	L	R		L
bll.chge:	shuffle:	hop:	step:	bll.chge:	shuffle:	hop:	step:	shuffle:	hop:	step	heelbt:	step	heelbt:		
a 3	a 4	a	5 a 6	a 7	a	8	a 1	&	a 2	&	a				

R		L	R	L		R		L	R	L		R
step	heelbt:	shuffle:	hop:	step	heelbt:	step	heelbt:	shuffle:	hop:	step	heelbt:	
3	&	a 4	&	a	5	&	a	6	&	a 7	&	a 8

Break

	L		R			L	L R	R	L	
Tap	step	heel-tap:	heelbt:	*(miss):*	shuffle	bll.chge	heelbt:	stamp:	*(miss):*	
&	a	1	<u>&</u>	*(2)*	a 3	& a	4	<u>&</u>	*(5)*	

```
     R    L    R
Shuffle: hop: step heelbt: (miss):
  a  6   &   a   7      (8)
```

234 Vocabulary check: Shuffle spring working on levels of tone.
  Tempo: Between 112 and 124.
  Music: CD.16(6) (12): CD.15(7): CD.1(3)(6): CD.2(1): CD.6(2) (4).

Using shuffle spring. The shuffle is at the back and the body leans slightly forwards. If using a side shuffle, the weight will be over the toes but the body will be more upright. Keep the rhythm evenly spaced between the beat. First practise it keeping the same light tone throughout the eight counts. Then, by landing on a dry knee, introduce accents on some of the counts.

Shuffle spring even tone
&a1&a2 &a3&a4&a5&a6&a7&a8

Then add accents as follows:
&a<u>1</u> &a2 &a<u>3</u> &a4 &a<u>5</u> &a6&a7&a8

Then change the accents to:
 &a1&a<u>2</u> &a3 &a<u>4</u> &a5&a<u>6</u> &a7&a8

Then to:
&a<u>1</u>&a2&a3&a<u>4</u>&a5&a6&a<u>7</u> (miss).

Try also taking the whole sequence on a very light tone, then medium and then heavy.
Take the exercise, each student travelling backwards separately on diagonal. It can be taken as four separate exercises, or the four phrases could be taken consecutively, dancing each once through each.
The exercises could also be taken starting on the count of 1, making the accent on the forward tap of the shuffle. It could be taken with a side shuffle or a back shuffle.

235 Vocabulary check: shim sham exercise: Shim sham(170).
  Tempo: 111–214.
  Music suggestion: CD.16(10) = 174: CD.1(12) = 194: CD.18(1) = 111: (15) = 210: (7) = 214:
  CD.12(10) = 182 (but if using this track start on count '1' and take all the steps one count later).

```
Commence R          Commence L               R                   L
Shim sham:          shim sham:         stamp(n) pu step heelbt: stamp(n) pu step heelbt:
8+12+34+5+6+7       8+12+34+5+6+7       8      + 1    +   2      +  3   +
```

```
   R         R          L        R            L
stamp(n) pu step heelbt: step heelbt: step heelbt: stamp(n) pu step heelbt:
   4      + 5  +     6   +     7   +    8      + 1  +
```

```
        R                       L              R
stamp(n) pu step heelbt: (miss): step heelbt: stamp(n)  pu step heelbt: (miss):
   2      + 3   +    (4)   +    5   ±      6  + 7      (8)
```

236 Vocabulary check: One and two sounds and 12th notes (N.B. stomp(no.28))
Tempo: From 117–162.
Music suggestion: CD.1(3) = 117: (6) = 120: (9) = 131: (11) = 128: CD.2(1) = 120: (4) = 162: CD.6(2) = 124.

Move to RS on first six counts.

R	L	L(tog)	R(toRS)		L	R	L	R	L
Tap step:	(sd)shuffle:	bll.chge:			chug:	chug:	chug:	chug:	pu step:
a	1	a 2	a 3		a	4	a	5	a 6

R	R(tog)	L(toLS)		R	L	R		L		L	R
(sd)shuffle	bll.chge:			chug:	chug:	chug:	*(miss):*	stamp(n):	pu step:	stamp(n):
a 7	a 8			a	1	&	*(2)*	a̲	3 a	4̲

R	L	R	L	R		R		R(toRS)	L	R	L(ft.tog)
pu:	heelbt:	toe tap:	heelbt:	toe tap:		toe-beat:	*(miss)*	tap step:	bll.chge:		step:
a	5	&	a	6		&	*(7)*	a 8	& 1	2

R(toRS)	L	R	L(face RS)			R			L(toRS)
Tap step:	bll.chge:		flap:	clap *(miss):*	tap step	stomp:	*(miss):*	clap:	step:
a	3	& 4	a 5	&̲ *(6)*	a 7	&	*(8)*	a	1

Travel backwards to L S

R	L	R	L		R	L	R	L(sd)	R(XfL to face front)
Shuffle:	hop:	step:	step	heelbt:	shuffle:	hop:	step:	bll.	chge	*(miss)*
a 2	a 3	a 4			a 5	a 6	a 7			*(8)*

237 Vocabulary check: Shuffle step heelbt – for simple close work.
Tempo: 145 to 200.
Music suggestion: CD.16(2) = 170: CD.3(1) = 192: CD.1(1) = 169: (4) = 145: (8)=200: CD.8(6) = 178: CD.12(3) = 170: CD.18(6) = 176:

R	R(bsdL)	R	L	R(toRS)
(sd)shuffle	step	heelbt:	heelbt:	tap step heelbt: repeat to LS
1 +	2	+	3	+ 4 + 5 + 6 + 7 + 8 +

R	R(bsdL)	R	L	R	R(bsdL)	R	L	R
(sd)shuffle	step	heelbt:	heelbt:	(sd)shuffle	step	heelbt:	heelbt:	tap step heelbt chug:
1 +	2	+	3	+ 4	+	5	+ 6	+ 7 ±̲

238 Vocabulary check: Tap-step heelbt. Shuffles for simple close work.
Tempo: Start slowly – increase tempo to approximately 200 eventually.
Music: CD.18(6) = 176: CD.3(1) = 192: CD.1(1) = 169: (4) = 117: (8) = 200: CD.8(6) = 178: CD.12(3) = 170.

   R(toRS)   L   R(tog)   L   R(to RS)   L
Tap-step heelbt: heelbt: ball dig: heelbt: tap-step heelbt: heelbt:
 +   1   +   2   3   4   +   5   +   6

    R(tog)   L   R(toRS)   L   R   L
pu step heelbt: heelbt: tap-step heelbt: heelbt: heelbt: heelbt:
 +   7   +   8   +   1   +   2   +   3

    R(tog)   L   R
pu step heelbt: shuffle step heelbt: stamp(w): repeat L: (or stamp(n)repeat same foot)
 +   4   +   5 + 6   +   7

239 Vocabulary: Exactly the same steps as No. 238, but change the rhythm.
    Tempo: 117 to 200.
    Music: CD.3(1) = 192: CD.1(4) = 117: (8) = 200: CD.12(3) = 170: CD.18(6) = 176: CD.8(6) = 178.

   R(toRS)   L   R(tog)   L   R(to RS)   L   R(tog)   R
Tap-step heelbt: heelbt: *(miss)* ball.dig: heelbt: tap-step heelbt: heelbt: pu step: *(miss)*: heelbt:
 1   +   2   ±   *(3)*   +   4   5   +   6   +   7 ±   *(8)*   +

 L   R(toRS)   L   R   L   R   R(tog)   L   R
Heelbt: tap-step heelbt: heelbt: heelbt: heelbt: pu:*(miss)*:step heelbt: shuffle step heelbt: stamp:
 1   e   +   a   2   +   3   ± *(4)*   +   5   6 e +   a   7

240 Vocabulary check: Simple one- and two-sound steps. Toe drag (optional).
    Tempo: 106 to 137.
    Music: CD.16(4) = 106: (12) = 113: CD.15(12) = 137: CD.1(3) = 117: (6) = 120: (9) = 131:
    CD.6(2) = 124: (4) = 107.

      R   R L   R L R   L   R
(st)shuffle (sd)shuffle (st)shuffle: bll.chge: *(miss)*: bll.chge shuffle: hop: step:
  a 1   a 2   a 3 a 4   *(5)*   a 6   a 7 a 8

L(Xf) R(toRS)   L(bR) R   L(to side)   R(bL) L R(to side)   L(toLS)
Step: tap step: bll.chge: stamp(w): *(miss)*: bll.chge: stamp(w): *(miss)*: step heelbt:
  1   a 2   a 3   &   *(4)*   a 5   &   *(6)*   a   7

R(toLCF) L R   L   R(turnL)   L   R (XL)   L (toLS)
tap step: bll.chge: step: step: step: step heelbt: *(miss)*: step heelbt:
 a 8   a 1   2   3   4   5 &   *(6)*   a   7

   R(toRS)   L(bR)   R   L(toLS)   R(bL)   L(w.R toe drag through to front)
Step heelbt: toe tap: heelbt: step: toe-beat: *(miss)*: heelbt(drag R toe across)
 8   a   1   a   2   &   *(3)*   4

     L   R   L

(miss) hop: heel-dig ball-beat: toe-tap: *(miss)*.
  (5)   a   6   a   7   *(8)*

241 Vocabulary check: Brush step heelbt scuff(31) : stomp(28).
     Tempo: 107.
     Music suggestion: CD.6(4) = 107.

The step has an action similar to a pendulum.

        R   L(toLS)   R(XbL)   L(toLS)

(bk)brush step heelbt: step heelbt: (bk)brush step heelbt: (flt)scuff: *(miss)*:
    a   1   &   a   2   &   a   3   <u>&</u>   *(4)*

Repeat twice – commencing L and then R a5&a6&a7<u>&</u> *(8)* a1&a2&a3<u>&</u> *(4)*

Break

        L   R(fwd)   both(tog)   R(fwd)   L(toLCF)

(bk)brush step: stamp: *(miss)*: jump(feet tog): stomp: *(miss)*: (or scuff to repeat)
    a   5   <u>&</u>   *(6)*   a   <u>7</u>   *(8)*   8

242 Vocabulary check: Shuffle: 2s.hop: one-sound steps: 12th notes and 8th note triplets.
     Tempo: 112–131.
     Music: CD.16(12) = 113: CD.1(3) = 117: (9) = 131: CD.2(2) = 151: CD.6(2) = 124.

 R   L   R(XfL)   L(bR)   R

Tap spring: tap step: shuffle step heelbt: shuffle step heelbt: (bk)shuffle spring:
a   1   a   2   a 3   &   a   4 &   a   5   & a   6

        L   R   L   R(bL)   L   R

(bk)shuffle spring: 3s.shuffle: 2s.hop: step heelbt: stamp: *(miss)*: (bk)brush step heelbt:
  & a   7   n & a   8 &   a   1   <u>&</u>   *(2)*   &   a   3

L(sdwys)   R((bL)   L   R   L   R   R(toRS)

stamp: (bk)brush step heelbt: stamp: *(miss)*: heel-dig pu: 2s.hop: (sd)shuffle toe tap   step:
 <u>&</u>   a   4   &   <u>a</u>   *(5)*   a   6   & a   7 &   a   8

Repeat L

243 Vocabulary check: Paddle and roll(124). Step-heelbt(128).
     Tempo: Start 108 and build to 140 eventually.
     Music: CD.16(3) = 108: CD.11(3) = 133: CD.3(3) = 140 fast.

'Paddle and roll' is one of the basic steps used in rhythm tap and close work, and many rhythms and steps can be developed from it. The most natural rhythms are '1e+a' or 'e+a1'. If the music is very fast these could be taken to '1+2+3+4+' or '+8+1+2+3', and so on. Another useful step for fast tap is 'step heelbt'(128) taken as one movement. The following exercise uses these two steps with a basic rhythm in order to concentrate on developing relaxation and speed of footwork.

R	L	R(toRS)	L(feet tog)	R(to RS)	L(feet tog)
Paddle:	paddle:	step heelbt:	step heelbt:	step heelbt:	step heelbt
1 e + a	2 e + a	3 e	+ a	4 e	+ a

Repeat twice   1 e + a 2 e + a 3 e + a 4 e + a 1 e + a 2 e + a 3 e + a 4 e + a

Break

R	L	R
Paddle:	paddle:	stamp:
5 e + a	6 e + a	<u>7</u>

244 Vocabulary check: One and two sounds and syncopation.
   Tempo: 124 or 128 to 104–116.
   Music: CD.15(13) = 126: (12) = 137: CD.16(7) = 145: CD.2(2) – first part of track only = 151 (it changes to waltz).

R		L	R	L		R		L	R
Tap step:		tap step:	tap step:	tap step heelbt:		stamp(n) pu step:		stamp(n) pu step:	stamp(w)
a	1	a 2	a 3	a 4	a	<u>5</u>	a 6	<u>a</u>	7 a <u>8</u>

L		R	L		R		L		L	R
Tap spring:		tap spring:	tap spring:		shuffle step heelbt:		stamp(n):	( )	pu step heelbt:	stamp(n)
a	1	a 2	a 3	a 4	& a	<u>5</u>	( ) a 6	&	<u>a</u>	

R		L	R		L	R		L(XfR)		R(bk)
pu step heelbt:		stamp(n) pu:	hop:		(bk)shuffle step:	pu spring:		shuffle step:		step heelbt:
7 &	a	<u>8</u>	a 1	& a	2	a 3	& a	4	& a	

L		L R	L		R		L		R	L	R
Stamp(n) ( ) pu:		hop:	tap spring:		stamp(n) pu step:		stamp(n) pu step:		(sd)shuffle:	hop:	toe tap:
<u>5</u>	( ) a 6	&	a	<u>7</u>	& a	<u>8</u>	& a	1 &	a	2	

L	R	L	R		R		L		R	
heelbt:	toe tap:	heelbt:	toe beat:	*(miss)*	stamp(n) pu step:		stamp(n) pu step:		stamp(w) chug:	
&	a	3	<u>&</u>	*(4)*	<u>a</u>	5 &	<u>a</u>	6 &	<u>a</u>	<u>7</u>

245 Vocabulary check: Shuffle step heelbt: 3s.riff(fwd)(bk): sideways travelling step.
   Tempo: From 73 to 137 or quicker.
   Music: CD.15(2) = 73: (8) = 76: (13) = 119: CD.1(3) = 117: (6) = 120: CD.2(1) = 120: CD.18(4) = 94: (5) = 137.

Travel sideways to LS

R(b)		L(toLS)		R		R(XfL)		R(XfL)	
Shuffle step heelbt:		tap step heelbt:		3s.open.riff(fwd):		3s.open.riff(bk):		step heelbt:	
8 &	a	1	& a	2	& a 3		& a 4		& a	

113

	L	R	L	R		L		R	L	
Toe tap:	heelbt:	toe tap:	heelbt:	tap step	heelbt:	pu:	heelbt:	*repeat ad lib.*
5	&	a	6	& a	7	&	a

246 Vocabulary check: 4s.cramp roll: 3s.shuffle: paddle: scuffle.
  Tempo: = From 74 to 92.
  Music: CD.15(8) = 76: CD.14d(2) = 74: CD.14b(6) = 82.

R(b)	L(Xf)	R(toRCF)			L		R
Shuffle step:	step heelbt:	heel-dig ball-beat:	(sd)shuffle step heelbt:	stamp(w):
& a	1 & a	2	&	a 3	& a	4

L(XbR)	R(sdwys)	L(ft.tog)			R		
pu step heelbt:	stamp:	( )	step heelbt:	stamp(n):	(flt)scuff:	(jump into)4s.crmp.rl:
& a 5	&	(-)	6 &	a	7	nna8 (-)

R	L	R	L	R	L		R(wide to RS)
Paddle:	stamp(w):	step heelbt:	3s.shuffle:	heelbt:	step heelbt:		stamp(w):
a1&a	2	& a	3 n n	n	n a	4

			L	R	R	L	L	R
Drag LF twds RF – straighten and rising on RF:	bll.chge:	hop into scuffle:	ball beat:	ball dig:
(5).			a	6	n	n n	a	7

The last ball dig with weight to repeat on left foot or without weight to repeat on same foot.

247 Vocabulary check: Paddle(124): cahito(132).
  Tempo: 120–230.
  Music: CD.8(7) = 125: (9) = 135: (8) = 200: CD.12(8) = 193: CD.1(5) = 228.

N.B. Leave the LF on the floor for the repeat.

	L	R	L	R	L	R	L	R	L
Heelbt:	(sd)paddle:	heelbt:	(sd)paddle:	heelbt:	(sd)paddle:	(sd)paddle:	heelbt:	(sd)paddle:
1	+ 2 + 3	4	+ 5 + 6	7	+ 8 + 1	+ 2 + 3	4	+ 5 + 6

(travelling backwards)

R	L	R	L	R	L	R	L	R	L	L	R
heelbt:	paddle:	paddle:	paddle:	paddle:	paddle:	stamp(w):	step:	cahito:	cahito:	heelbt:	stamp:
7	+8+1	+2+3	+4+5	+6+7	+8+1	2		3	+ 4 +	5 + 6	+	7

248 Vocabulary: Paddles (124).
  Tempo: = 165 develop to 194.
  Music: CD.8(9) = 135: CD.12(8) = 193: CD.1(5) = 228: (8) = 200: CD.14a(1) = 203: (9) = 212.

	L	R	L	R		L		R
Heelbt:	paddle:	heelbt:	paddle:	tap step heelbt:	step:
1	+ 2 + 3	4	+ 5 + 6	7 +	8	+

Repeat commencing RF   1+2+3 4+5+6 7+8+
Repeat commencing LF   1+2+3 4+5+6 7+8+

Break

R	L	R	L		R	L
Heelbt:	paddle:	paddle:	stamp(n):	*(miss)*:	heelbt:	stamp(w):
1	+2+3	+4+5	<u>+</u>	*(6)*	+	<u>7</u>

249 Vocabulary check: Paddle(124). 4s.riff(76): 6s.riff(78): sngl.trav(130).
  Tempo: From 134 to 212.
  Music: CD.8(9) = 135: CD.12(8) = 193: CD.1(1) = 169: (4) = 145: (8) = 200: CD.14a(9) = 212.

	R(toRS)		L		R(tog)				
Tap step	heelbt:	heelbt:	pu	step	heelbt:	repeat commencing LF:	repeat starting RF		
1	+	2	+	3	+	4	+5+6+7+	8+1+2+3	

L	R		L		R		L	R	L	L		R(ft.tog)
6s.riff:	paddle:		stamp(n)	pu step:	stamp(n)	pu step:	4s.riff:	chug:	chug:	chug:	*(miss)*:	step heelbt
+4+5+6 +7+8	<u>+</u>		1	+	<u>2</u>		+ 3	+4+5	+	6	<u>+</u> *(7)*	+ 8

	L(bR)		R(turned in)	(turned out)	(in)		(out)	
Shuffle step	heelbt:		stamp(w):	ball beat	heelbt		ball beat(sngl.trav)	
+ 1	+	<u>2</u>	<u>+</u>	3	+		4	

L		L(turned out)		(in)	(out)	(straight)	R(fwd)
Stamp(w):	*(miss)*:	ball beat(sngl.trav):	heelbt:	ball beat:	heelbt:	stamp:	
<u>+</u>	*(5)*	+		6	+	7	<u>+</u>

250 Vocabulary check: 7s.riff: paddle: 3s.shuffle.
  Tempo: = 96.
  Music suggestion: CD.15(9) = 71 to start: CD.1(7) = 107: CD.5(1) = 78: CD.14a(10) = 133:
  CD.14b(6) = 82: CD.17(9) = 107.

Use the naturally heavy sounds to create subtle accents.

L	R	L	R	L	R		L	R	L	R	L
Heelbt:	shuffle:	heelbt:	toe tap:	heelbt:	7s.riff:		shuffle:	heelbt:	toe tap:	heelbt:	7s.riff:
1	& a	2	&	a	3&a4&a5	& a	6	&	a	7&a8&a1	

	R		L		R		L	R	L	R
(sd) shuffle step	heelbt:		paddle:		(sd)shuffle step	heelbt:	paddle:	3s.shuffle:	heelbt:	toe tap:
& a	2	&	a 3 & a		4 &	a	5	& a 6 &	a 7 &	a 8

251 Vocabulary: Paddles using doubling-up.

> **Tempo:** = 100 initially and then gradually increase the speed
>
> **Music:** CD.10(6) = 129: eventually CD.11(10) = 133 for practice.

An exercise in doubling the timing. Start with even eight notes, taking a simple exercise with heelbts, paddle and roll and step heelbt. This is taken through twice to the even 8th note rhythm. This takes four bars of 4/4 music. Then the same exercise is taken three times to the 16th note rhythm. This takes three bars of 4/4 music. A stamp and a tacit to finish. Here you will see both sets of counts, written one under the other, showing where it translates from 8ths to the doubled rhythm. Notice that 'e' of the 16th notes is missing between the 2nd and 3rd beats and between the 6th and 7th beats.

1 + 2 + 3 ( ) 4 + 5 + 6 + 7 + 8 + 1 + 2 + 3 ( ) 4 + 5 + 6 + 7 + 8 + 1

1 e + a 2 ( ) + a 3 e + a 4 e + a 5 e + a 6 ( ) + a 7 e + a 8 e + a 1

	L		R		L			R		L	
Heelbt:	paddle:		step heelbt:		paddle:			paddle:			
1		+ 2 +	3		4		+		5 + 6 +	7 + 8 +	

Leave RF on floor ready for heelbt to repeat on opposite foot.

1 + 2 + 3 4 + 5 + 6 + 7 + 8 +

Take the second set of counts and repeat exactly the same step at twice the speed:

	L	R		L	R	L	R	L
Heelbt:	paddle:	*( )*	step heelbt:	paddle:	paddle:	repeat twice – R then L:		
1	e+a2	*(e)*	+	a	3e+a	4e+a	5e+a6(e)+a7e+a8e+a	1e+a2(e)+a3e+a4e+a

R		R		R			R	L
Stamp(n):		stamp(n):		stamp(n):		*(miss)*:	step:	paddle:
<u>5</u>		<u>+</u>		<u>6</u>		(+)	7	e + a 8

252 Vocabulary check: 3s.shuffle: paddles (with different rhythms): 4s.riff.

> **Tempo:** = 104.
>
> **Music:** Ellington CD.2(4) = 84: CD.10(6)= 129 eventually.

R (XfL)			L		R		L			R	L	R	
Shuffle step heelbt:		heelbt:		pu step heelbt:		paddle:		*(miss)*:	chug:	chug:	chug:		
1 +		2		+	3		+ 4		+	5 + 6<u>+</u>	*(7)*	+	8	+

L	R (sdwys toR)		L(tog)		R(sdwys toR)		L(tog)		R		L
Paddle:	tap step heelbt:		step heelbt:		tap step heelbt:		pu step heelbt:		3s.shuffle:		heelbt:
1 e+a	2	+	3	+	4	+ 5	+	6 +	7	e + a	8

R	L	R	L		R	L	L(diag.bk)	R	L	R
4s.riff:	pad( )dle:	4s.riff:	toe-tap:	*(miss)*:	heelbt:	toe-tap:	step:	*(miss)* paddle:	paddle:	paddle:
e+a1	2+(3)+4	e+a5	<u>+</u>	*(6)*	+	7	<u>+</u>	*(8)* 1e+a	2e+a	3e+a

	L		L	R	L	R		L	L

stamp(w): heelbt: shuffle: heelbt: toe-tap step: *(miss)*: heel tap: heelbt:

| 4 | | 5 | e + | a | 6 | + | *(7)* | + | 8 |

253 Vocabulary: Using riff with hop or hop heel (85–87).
   Tempo: = 100 (or quicker).
   Music: CD.15(3) = 116 eventually: CD.1(3) = 117: (7) = 107: CD.2(2) = 151: CD.5(8) = 120: CD.14b(10) = 127.

| | R | L | | R | | L | | R | R L | L | R | L | R(b) |

Shuffle: hop: 6s.(hop.heel) riff : paddle(sd): shuffle bll.chge: heelbt: shuffle: hop: step:

| 1 | & | a | 2 & a 3 & | a | 4 & a 5 | & a | 6 & | a | 7 & | a | 8 |

Repeat twice on the same foot starting each with: (bk)tap spring(LF) & a

Break

| | L R L | | | R | R L | L | R | L(turning R) | R |

Shuffle spring (three times): shuffle bll.chge heelbt: step: 5s.crmp.rl chge: step chug:

| & a 1 | & a 2 | & a 3 | & a | 4 & | a | 5 | & a 6 & a | 7 | <u>&</u> |

254 Vocabulary check: 3s.shuffle, 5s. and 6s.riff: paddle.
   Tempo: 100 to 130.
   Music: CD.8(4) = 104 when counted half time. CD.12(2) = 129 (after practice).

| L | | R(sd) | L | | R | | L | | R | L |

Heelbt: 3s.shuffle: heelbt: 6s.riff: heelbt: *(miss)*: heelbt: paddle:

| 1 | | e + a | 2 | + 3 + 4 + 5 | <u>+</u> | *(6)* | 7 | e + a 8 |

| R | | L | R | R L | L | | R |

6s.riff: pu step heelbt: shuffle: bll.chge: heelbt: *(-)* 5s.riff:

| e + a 1 e + | a | 2 | e | + | a | 3 | e | + | *(-)* 4 e + a 5 |

| | L | R | L |

Step heelbt: paddle: stamp(w) chug:

| + | a | 6 e + a | 7 | <u>+</u> |

To repeat on the opposite foot take shuffle step (RF) 'e+a', and then the heelbt (RF) to start the new phrase on '1'. To repeat on the same foot, take a 3s.shuffle on the counts 'e+a', and then the heelbt (LF) to start the new phrase.

255 Vocabulary check: Paddle: 3s.shuffle: rippledown.
    Tempo suggestion: = 100.
    Music: CD.15(6) = 76: (9) = 71: CD.1(7) = 107: CD.5(1) = 78: (8) = 120.

Commence feet apart

R	L	R(toRS)	L	R	L(toLS)	R	L
Pu step heelbt:	paddle:	stamp:	pu step heelbt:	paddle:	stamp:	pu step heelbt:	3s shuffle:
a 1 &	a2&a	<u>3</u>	& a 4	&a5&	<u>a</u>	6 & a	7&&

R	L(leave R down)	R	L(toLS)	R	L	R	L(toLS)
heelbt:	step heelbt:	heelbt:	stamp:	(bk)tap step:	stamp:	(bk)tap step heelbt:	stamp:
a	8 &	a	<u>1</u>	& a	<u>2</u>	& a 3	<u>&</u>

R(leave LF down)	L	R(to R)	L	R	L	R
(bk)tap step heelbt:	heelbt:	(flt)drop:	shuffle pu.chge:	toe tap	rippledown:	chug:
a 4 &	a	<u>5</u>	nnna	6	nnna7	<u>+</u>

256 Vocabulary check: 5s.paddle: 6s.riff.
    Tempo: Suggestion crotchet = start at 84 and work up to about 104 (straight time).
    Music suggestion: CD.6(8) = 78: CD.12(4) = 136: CD.2(3) = 139 eventually.

L	R	L	R	L	R	L	R	L	
Heelbt:	paddle:	*( )* heelbt:	5s.paddle:	paddle:	heelbt:	5s.paddle:	heelbt:	6s.riff:	repeat RF
1	e + a 2	*(e)* +	a 3 e + a	4 e + a	5	e + a 6 e	+	a 7 e + a 8	

257 Vocabulary check: Paddles: press cramp roll.
    Tempo suggestion: = 182.
    Music suggestion: CD.12(14) = 136: CD.2(9) = 221.

L	R	R	L	R
Heelbt:	paddle:	press crmp.rl:	paddle:	paddle
1	+ 2 + 3	4nna	5 + 6 +	7 + 8 +

Leave LF on ground to repeat same foot   1 + 2 + 3 4nna 5 + 6 + 7 + 8 +
Repeat once more on same foot   1+ 2 + 3 4nna 5 + 6 + 7 + 8 +

Break

L	R	L	R	L
Heelbt:	paddle:	step heelbt:	paddle:	step heelbt *(miss)*:
1	+2+3	+ 4	+5+6	+ 7 *(8)*

258 Vocabulary check: Hopping-riff: ball-heel-turn: waltz clog.
    Tempo: = From 94 to 166.
    Music: CD.18(4) = 94: CD.5(8–13) = 120: CD.15(10) = 166.

```
     R              R            L       R       L   R(XfL)
Triple half break:  7s.hopping.riff: (miss): pu step: shuffle: hop: step:
1 & a 2 & a 3 & a   4 a 5 & a 6  &    (7)    a 8    a 1    &     a
```

```
  R   L  R  L              R    L      R  L(XbR)      R(toRCF)
Heel heel ball ball (turn.L): (miss): step: shuffle: hop: step:    waltz clog (dble)
  2    & a 3              (4)    a    5 &    a     6         & a 7 & a 8
```

259 Vocabulary check: Heel-ball turn.
Tempo: = 70 (for practice, and work up to 120 or more).
Music: CD.15(11) = 70: CD.18(4) = 94: CD.1(7) = 107: CD.5(8) = 120: CD.6(12) = 121.

Italic brackets have been inserted between some of the counts as a reminder to give full value to the silence. It is often 'between' the beat that students hurry the rhythm.

The sequence travels sideways from LCB to RCF
```
   R     R  L  L           R                L
Shuffle bll.chge heelbt:  8s.hop.heel.riff: ( )   paddle(sd):
1  &   a  2    &     a 3 & a 4 & a 5   ( )   6 & a 7
```

```
   R      R L  L     R    R L  L
stamp(n) pu: bll.chge heelbt:  shuffle bll.chge heelbt:
  &      a 8 &    a    1 &   a  2     &
```

```
      R          R(XfL)   R   R  L         R   L      R
2s.open.riff.fwd ( ) 2s.riff (bk) step:  heel heel (miss)  ball ball turn: chug: (miss)
   a      3     ( )   4 &    a   5   &   (6)    a   7       &    (8)
```

260 Vocabulary check: Heel ball turn (outwards): single travel interrupted by a step.
Tempo: = 92 (waltz time).
Music: CD.21(6) = 107: (9) = 135: CD.22 = 134.

Face RCF. RF in front
```
     R    L      R(XbL)        L(fwd to RCF)
(bk)brush: hop: shuffle step heelbt:  heel-dig ball-beat:
    a    1    & a   2    &       a    3
```

```
     R        L                 L        R      L(XfR)
Tap step heelbt: toe tap (turn to R): (miss): step: tap spring heelbt: stamp(n)
&   a    4      &            (5)     a  6 &    a        1
```

```
L  R  L  R  L  R        L(b)            R(fwd) L(to LCF)
pu: hop: shuffle: hop: toe tap: hop:  step heelbt: (miss): spring:  scuff(flt):
a  2  & a 3    &    a    4   &      (5)     a       6
```

Repeat L. Repeat R, but finish with step bll.chge R L on count 'a 6'.

Break

R	L	R(bk)	L	R(XfL)
Toe-tap:	2s.hop:	shuffle step:	pu spring:	shuffle step heelbt:
&	a 1	& a 2	& a	3 & a 4

L	R(turn out)	L(b)	R(turn in)	R(turn out)	L(toL)
heelbt:	ball beat:	step:	heelbt	ball beat:	ball dig:
&	a	5	&	a	6

	L	R	L	R(b)	R	L	R
(miss):	hop:	shuffle:	hop:	step:	heel:	heel:	ball (turn R) (miss)
(1)	2	n &	a	3	a	4	& (5 6)

Either finish on the count of '4', or take two steps back L R ready to repeat the sequence commencing with LF.

261 Vocabulary: 5s.riff: rippledown: clp.pll.bk.1ft.
Tempo: From 120 to 140.
Music: CD.12(2) = 121: (20) = 139: CD.2(3) = 139.

R		R L	R	L	R(to face LS)
Shuffle (miss) bll.chge:		5s.riff:	pu step:	shuffle step heelbt:	
1 ± (2)	+	3 (-) + a 4 +	5 (-) 6	+ 7 + 8	+

L(fwd to LS)		L	R(bL)	R(sdys to front)		R	L(faceLS)
Heel-dig ball beat:	(miss):heelbt:	toe tap:	ball dig:	(miss)	heelbt:	stamp(n) ( ):	
1	+	(2) +	3	±	(4) +	5	( )

(turn L) L	R(to front)	R(toRS)	L	L(toR)	L R	R
pu step heelbt:	stamp(n):	stamp(w):	pu:	clip:	bll.chge:	heelbt:
+ a 6	±	7	e	+	a 8	+

	Both feet(faceRS)		R		L	R	L
Simultaneous	chug twice:	stomp:	(miss):	rippledown:	heelbt:	heel dig ball beat:	
	1 2	±	(3)	n n a 4	+	5	+

R(sdwys to RCF)	L(bsdR)	R(sdwys)	L(bsdR)	R(sdwys)
step heelbt:	step heelbt:	step heelbt:	step heelbt:	step heelbt:
6 +	7 e	+ a	8 e	+ a

L(to RCF)	R	L	R	L	R
3s.shuffle:	heelbt:	toe tap:	heelbt:	step heelbt:	heelbt:
1 e +	a	2	e	+ a	3

	L	R	L	R		R
3s.shuffle:	heelbt:	step heelbt:	heelbt:	(miss):		clp.pll.bk.1ft.heelbt:
e + a	4	e +	5	(6)		nnna7

262 Bosanova with Jo and Friends

Vocabulary: Mainly close-work steps with opportunities for improvisation.

Tempo: = 122.

Music: CD.7(13).

The following sequence can be used in various ways. Each section 'A to K' can be used as a separate exercise. Alternatively the whole piece could be danced as a solo or group, with or without improvisation. If taken as a group, the improvisation could be solo or group efforts.

Introduction: Four bars – wait.

Section A

R		L(bR)		R			L	
Heel-dig ball beat:		step:		heel-dig ball beat:	*(miss)*:		step heelbt:	
1		2		3	4	+	(5)	+	6

	R			L		R(bL)		L	
stamp(n) pu step heelbt:			stamp(w):		*(miss)*	step:		stamp(n) pu step:	
±	7	+	8	±		(1)	2	±	3	+

R(toRS):	L(bR)	R(toRS)		L	(take RL to RS)		R			L	
stamp(w):	step:	stamp(w):	step:		*(miss)*:		(bk)brush step: clap:			step: clap:	
4	+	5	±		(6)		+	7	+	8	+

R(XfL)	L(toLS)	R(XfL)		L(toLS)	R(XfL)	L(to LS)	R(toRS)
Stamp(w):	step:	stamp(w):	*(miss)*:	step:	stamp(w):	step heelbt:	step heelbt:
1	2	±	(3)	+	4	5 +	6 +

L(XfR)	R(toRS)	L(XfR)		R(toRS)	L(XfL)	R(toRS)
Stamp(w):	step:	stamp(w):	*(miss)*:	step:	stamp(w):	step heelbt:
7	8	±	(1)	+	2	3 +

L(toLS)		R(bk):	L(tog)	R(fwd)
step heelbt:	*(miss)*:	step:	step:	stamp:
4	±	(5)	+	6	7

Repeat the first six bars of **Section A** 1234+*(5)*+6±7+8± *(1)*2±3+4+5±*(6)*+7+8± 1 2±*(3)*+4 5+6+7 *(8)*

L(toLCF)	R L			R L		
Step:	bll.chge:	(turning L):	bll.chge:	(turning L):	*(pause dragging RF to L)*	
1	2 +	(3)	4 5		(6 7)	

Section B

Italic brackets (-) have been used to denote which part of the 16th note is silent.

R	R(b)	L		R		L		R	
Shuffle toe-beat:	heelbt:	step heelbt:		heelbt:		stamp(n) pu step heelbt:			
8 +	1	+	2		+	3	±	4 +	5

```
        L             R      L                    L
stamp(n)  pu step heelbt:  step heelbt: stamp(n):  (miss):  shuffle step heelbt:
  ±      6   e    +    a   7      ±        (8)     1 e   +   a
```

```
  R          L            R                  L           R
5s.paddle:   7s.riff:     stamp(n) chug:  (miss): shuffle step heelbt: heelbt: (miss):
2 e + a 3  e + a 4 e +a       5      ±     (6)     e  +    a     7      ±      (8)
```

Repeat **Section B** commencing L (or improvise for four bars).

Section C

```
   R(XbL)     L        R(to RS)          L (XbR)              R(to RS)     L
Shuffle step: tap step: tap step heelbt: (bk)tap step heel-tap heelbt: tap step heelbt: heelbt:
  8 +    1   +   2   +    3    +         4   +     5    +    6  e   +    a
```

```
R  L      R     L                                              L
pu:  heelbt: toe-tap toe-beat: chug (toe drag on R – finish R lifted to LCF): chug: (miss)
7  +    8    +     1                                          ±     (2)
```

```
       R          LtoR          L(b)     R    L      R      L
Heel-dig ball-beat: ball-dig: (miss): step: pu step heelbt: step: pu step heelbt: (flt)scuff:
  +      3          ±     (4)    5   e  +   a      6 e  +    a           7
```

(make one complete turn to R on 5 e + a 6 e + a 7 then circle the L leg ready for repeat on LF)

Repeat first two bars of **Section C** 8 + 1 + 2 + 3 + 4 + 5 + 6e+a7 + 8 + (or improvise for two bars)

```
  L    R    L       R    L
Chug:  chug:  chug: (miss): chug:  chug:  (miss)
  1    2    +    (3)   4    5    (6 7 8 1)
```

Section D (to saxophone solo). *(Bars 2 to 7 turning, travel in circle clockwise from LCF to LCB.)*

```
                        Making half turn          bkwds along LOD
              R            L    R   L   R   L        R      R
Stamp(n) pu step heelbt: step heelbt: step: toe tap: hop: step: (miss): pll.bk: pll.bk
   2    e   +    a     3   +    4   +   5    +   (6)    nna7   nna8
```

```
  L    R   L    R              L          R          L           R
heelbt:  scuff:  heelbt: step: (miss): 4s.crmp.rl.chge.turn: step: 4s.crmp.rl.chge.turn: step:
  1    2    3    +   (4)        nna5       6          nna7         8
```

```
Face outside circle               Turn to R
  L    R   L(f)   R(sd)   L(b)  R(sd)  L   R  R L      R      L  R L
shuffle: hop: step: stamp(w):  step: stamp(w): step: pu: bll.chge: pu step heelbt: step: bll.chge:
  e  +   a   1    2       +      3      + 4 + 5    +    6   +      7  + 8
```

Facing LS travel fwd along LOD to LCB

	R(xfL)		L(xfR)		R	L	R	R(slide into scuff)	L

Shuffle step heelbt: shuffle step heelbt: heelbt: step: stamp(n):   stamp: heelbt:

   + 1   +   2   + 3   + 4   +   5   6   7   8

Travelling to RCF

R   L(XbR) R(sd) L(f) R(twds RCF)

step(turn dragging toe of L behind): *(miss)*:   step   bll. chge: 6s.riff:

1   *(2)*   3   a   4   a 5 + 6 7 8

   L   R (facing front)   L   Tog.

step: stamp(n) pu step heelbt: stamp(n) pu step *(miss)*: simultaneous chug chug:

1   2   + 3   +   4   + 5   *(6)*   7   8

   L   R   L   R   L   R   L

Step: shuffle step heelbt: shuffle step heelbt: step heelbt: step heelbt: step heelbt: step heelbt:

1   e +   a   2   e +   a   3   e   +   a   4   e   +   a   5

   R   R(slide into scuff w.)   L   R   L   R

Stamp(n):   stamp   heelbt: step: 4s.crmp.rl(controlled): ball-dig (grad. xfer wgt):

6   7   8   1   2 3 + 4   5

Section E
Improvise.

Section F

   R   L   R   L(XfR)   R   L   R

Shuffle: hop: shuffle step: (sd)shuffle step: 5s.(hopping)riff: step heelbt: step heelbt:

1   +   2   + 3   +   4 +   5   + 6 + 7 +   8   e   +   a

      L   R   L(Xf)   R   L (Xf)   R(bsdL) (both feet)

(sd)shuffle: hop: step: 5s.(hopping)riff: (sd)shuffle step heelbt: *(miss)*: step: chug chug

   1 e   + *(-)* 2   + 3 e + *(-)* 4 *(-)* + a   5   +   *(6)*   +   7   ±

Repeat commencing R (or improvise for four bars).

Section G
(Repeat of **Section B**, but twice commencing with the RF) (or improvise for four or eight bars).

Section H

   L   R   L   R   L   R   L

Heelbt: 5s.paddle: step heelbt: paddle: step heelbt: paddle: step heelbt: *(miss)*:

1   + 2 + 3 +   4   +   5 + 6 7   +   8   + 1 + 2   3   ±   *(4)*

   R   L   R   L

3s.shuffle: heelbt: step heelbt: 3s.shuffle:

   + 5 +   6   +   7   8 e +

123

Section K

```
  L    R    L    R    L    R        L       R    L R
Step: cahito: cahito: cahito: pu: heelbt: toe-tap: heelbt: step heelbt:  repeat commencing R
  1  + 2 + 3 + 4  + 5 + 6   +      7       +    8   +      1+2+3+4+5+6+7+8+


        L         R    L                           L R
Shuffle step heelbt: step heelbt: step heelbt:  repeat R:  (miss): bll.chge:
  1 e  +   a    2   +    3   +    4e+a5+6+   (7)    +  8


     L    R                       L        R(knee bent)
Heel-ball: toe-beat: start hop(dragging toe) land from hop: stamp(sdwys to front)
   1    2    +           (3)            4          5
```

CD Check List

CD.1 *Tap Music for Dances, Volume 1 Swingin' Tappin' & Jammin'* The David Leonhardt Trio

CD.2 *Music for Tap 1.5:* Sam Weber and Jerry Kalaf

CD.3 *Jim Taylor's T Taps Music* by Milton Nelson

CD.4 *'Spice Up Your Tap'* by Stuart Rush

CD.5 *Practise Your Tap*, Selection 2

CD.6 *Gone Tappin'*, The Tap Dance CD

CD.7 Rossmoyne Junior Concert 2001

CD.8 *HMV Rag* 7 24353 0432 3

CD.9 *HMV Boogie Woogie* 7 24352 5446 2

CD.10 *HMV Piano Jazz* 7 24352 775 2 5

CD.11 *HMV Latin Jazz* 7 24352 08842 2

CD.12 *Bosanova Only* DC 850702

CD.13. *A Decade of Calligraph*– Calligraph Records CLG CD 031

CD.14a White Box (four CDs) – Pulse PBXCD 405

CD.14b   "   "

CD.14c   "   "

CD.14d   "   "

CD.15 *Paper Moon* – Telarc Jazz 0 89408 33752 9

CD.16 Robbie Williams – *Chrysalis* 7 24353 68262

CD.17 *Sleepless in Seattle* – Original Motion Picture EPC 473594 2

CD.18 Winifred Atwell PLS CD 577

CD.19 Count Basie, *Essential Collection Essential Collection* PYCD 268

CD.20 Duke Ellington – *The Essential Collection* – Legacy – 0 7464 – 65841 – 5

CD.20a " " 1927–40

CD.20b " " 1947–52

CD.20c " " 1956–62

CD.21 Eva Cassidy – *Songbird* – G2 10045

CD.22 George Michael *Listen Without Prejudice* EPC 467295 2

CD.23 *Ragtime Memories* MCPS PLAT CD 660

CD.24 *The Glory of Gershwin* featuring Larry Adler 522 727 - 2

CD.25 *The Best of Erroll Garner* CD 67018

CD.26 Charlie Barnet, *Empress* RAJCD 898

CD.27 Claude Bolling – *Jazz in Paris*, Gatanes Jazz Productions 7 31454 81512 3

CD.28 *The Very Best of Fats Waller* RCAVictor 0 9026 63731 – 2 3

CDs 1 to **6** were made especially for tap dancers.

CDs 21 and **22**, although more suitable for jazz, have two good tap-dancing tracks.

CD.25 is sophisticated and suitable for the higher levels.

CDs 25 and **27** are particularly good for improvisation.

CDs 1, 2 and 3 are available from Hollywood Tap Mall.

CD.6 is available from The 8 & 1 Piano Company.

CD.5 is available from I.S.T.D.

CDs 4 and **7** are available from Second Spin, Bexhill.

The remainder are available from Second Spin or any good record shop.

8   SEQUENCES, ROUTINES AND FRIENDS' CONTRIBUTIONS

SEQUENCES

FRIENDS' CONTRIBUTIONS

Some of the friends who contributed sequences.
ABOVE RIGHT: Fred Strickler, whose 'Tap Concerto' is included in the collection of sequences. (Photograph by Lois Greenfield)
RIGHT: Joy Hewitt, enjoying a teaching session in France.
FAR RIGHT: David Needham, who has extensive experience as a choreographer.

✳ The B.S. Chorus (*see* p.147)
✳ The shim sham shimmy, Leonard Reed (*see* p.149)

263 Rag for Rosina, an excerpt
Music: Sid Phillips: flapper rag – HMV *Ragtime Jazz Collection*.
Tempo: Crotchet, approximately 224.
Vocabulary check: Maxi-ford: pull-backs: American roll. (*Type of pll.bk optional, i.e. nos 98, 99 or 100 – or separated wings – no. 120.*)

First Eight Bars

```
   L     R      LtoR    L     L     R      LtoR      L                R
Drop: shuffle: pu.chge: toe-tap drop: shuffle: pu.chge:  toe tap (miss) stomp
   1    + 2      n a    3     4    + 5      n a       6       (7)      8
```

```
   L     R      LtoR    L     L     R      LtoR      L              L R
Drop: shuffle: pu.chge: toe-tap drop:  shuffle: pu.chge:  toe tap: (miss): bll.chge:
   1    + 2      n a    3     4    + 5      n a       6       (7)      a 8
```

```
L(toLCF)   R(bL)   L(toLCF)   R(bL)  L(XfR)          L        R(toRCF)
Step heelbt:  step:   step heelbt:  step:   step  (miss) heelbt:   stamp(w):
   1     2      3       4     5       6       +     (7)      +          8
```

```
L(XfR)   R(toRS)        L(ft.apart)           both          R      L
Step:   step heelbt: (miss)  step heelbt: (miss):slide tog.w.clip:(miss) heelbt: heelbt:
   1       2    +      (3)     +    4       (5)        6        (7)    +     8
```

Second Eight

```
   R          L     R    L(bR)   R     L     R    L(fR)    R                  L
Heel.bt: (sd)shuffle: hop:  step:  step: shuffle: hop:  step:  spring: (sd)shuffle spring heelbt:
   1            + 2    +     3     4    + 5    +    6      7           + 8    +     1
```

```
       R      L    R(XbL)  L(toLS)    R(fwd.toLCF)    L(rock bk)          R(toLCF)
(sd)shuffle: hop:  step:    step:     heel-dig ball beat:  heelbt: (miss): heel-dig ball beat:
     + 2      +     3        4          5       6           +     (7)      +        8
```

```
     L(toLCF)         R    L(toR)   L     L      R     L(toR)   L
Drop(flt) hop stomp: (bk)shuffle: pu.chge: toe tap: drop(flt): shuffle: pu.chge: toe tap
     1    2    3        + 4    n    a      5     6      + 7     n     a       8
```

```
  L(fwd)          R   L(fwd)            L
Stamp(n): (miss): heelbt: stamp(w): (miss): heelbt:
   1     (2 3)    4       5      (6 7)     8
```

Third Eight (*Jaunty – travelling straight to front*)

```
    R(fwd)                 L     R                    L(toLS)  R(fwd)
Heel-dig ball beat: heel-dig ball beat: step (into lunge sideways): (miss):   bll.chge
   1       2         3      4     5                          (6 7)    + 8
```

Rosina showing the position on count '6' of the first phrase in 'Rag for Rosina'.

Rosina showing the step into a lunge sideways on the fifth count of the first phrase of the Third Eight of 'Rag for Rosina'.

```
    L(fwd)              R              L              R   R
Heel-dig ball beat: heel-dig ball beat heelbt:   American roll:   Chicago roll heelbt:
    1       2           3        4      5    6na7+8+1+2+3+4+5     +6+7 +8+1  +
```

```
        L   R   L   R   L   R   L
Continuous step heelbt for seven counts (in place or trav.bk in a small circle)
        2 + 3 + 4 + 5 + 6 + 7 + 8 +
```

Fourth Eight

```
  R(XfL)    L    R    L    R    L          R
Stamp(n): heelbt: stamp(n): heelbt: scuff: heelbt: (bk)brush step heelbt:
   1      2      3       4      5      6        +   7   +
```

```
        L            R           L   R     L    R   L(XfR)
(sd)shuffle spring: (sd)shuffle spring: (sd)shuffle hop: (sd)shuffle: hop: step heelbt:
   8 +    1        +2      +      3 + 4      +  5  +  6    +
```

```
   R    L   R(XfL)     L(bR)  R(toRS into drag turn)      L
(sd)shuffle: hop: step heelbt:  step:   step (dragging RF in turn):  step
   7 +  8    +    1      2      3        (4 5 6 7)         8
```

127

R		R	R	L	RtoL	R

Stamp(n): *(miss)*: 4s.crmp.rl: drop(flt): shuffle pu.chge: toe-tap step:

1   *(2)*   nna3 4   + 5 n a 6 7

Coda (Bridge in Full Version)

L	R	LtoR	R	L		R	L	RtoL	L	R

Drop(flt): shuffle: pu.chge: heelbt: toe tap: *(miss)*: stomp: shuffle: pu.chge: heelbt: toe tap:

<u>1</u>   + 2   e +   a   3   *(4)* 5   a 6 e +   a   7

		R		R		R	

(miss): jump: *(miss)*: pll.bk: *(miss)*: pll.bk: *(miss)*: step: *(miss)*:

(8) 1   *(2)* nna3 *(4)* nna5 *(6)* 7   *(8)*

264 Five's Fine, an excerpt

Music: Easy 5/4 from *Spice Up Your Tap* by Stuart Rush.
Tempo: Crotchet = 112.
Vocabulary check: 6s. hop heel riff: sntch.pull-backs: 2s.hop.

First Eight Bars

Turning R and travelling to RCF

R	L	RtoL	R		L	R	L	R(bk)

Drop(flt): shuffle: pu.chge: (fwd)brush spring: 5s.riff: toe tap: heelbt: step:

<u>1</u>   a 2   & a   3   a   4&a5a 1   a   2

Trav.to LCB   TurnR to face front

L	L	L R		L	R	L	R

Pllbk: pll.bk: bll.chge: tap step: toe beat: heelbt: toe tap:

nna3 nna4 a 5   a 1   a   2   &

L	R	R	L	R	L		R		L

Heel beat: toe tap toe beat: hop: step: shuffle step: stamp(n) pu step heelbt: stamp(n)

a   3   <u>&</u>   4   +   5 + 1 <u>+</u>   2 & a <u>3</u>

L	R	L(XfR)	R		L(bR)	R	L

pu heelbt: shuffle step: step *(dragging LRF in twds R)*: step heelbt: scuffle: step:

a 4   & a 5 <u>1</u>   *(2)*   a 3   & a 4

R		L	R	L	R	L(XbR)	R	L	R	L

scuffle ball-beat: (sd)shuffle: hop: toe-tap: 2s.hop: step: heel heel ball ball (turn R):

& a   5   & a 1   &   a 2 a   3 a 4 <u>&</u>

	R(XfL)	L(toLS)	R(toRS)	L	R(toRS)		R	L	R

(miss): step: stamp(w): step: pu step: stamp(w): *(miss)*: stomp: step: pu spring:

(5) a   <u>1</u>   &   a 2   <u>&</u>   *(3)* a   4 & a

L(fwd)   R(dragLbk)   L   R   R L(ft.tog) Both ft tog
stamp(w):   heelbt: step: scuff(flt): *(miss):* bllchge: chug (simultaneous):
<u>5</u>:   1   a   <u>2</u>   *(3)*   a 4   <u>5</u>

Second Eight

L(releaseRfwd)   R   L   R   L R(XfL)   L(toLS) R(XfL)
Hop: (bk)brush step pu step; (sd)shuffle: hop: stamp(w): tap step: stamp(w):
1   a 2 & a   3 & a   <u>4</u>   & a   <u>5</u>

      L(toLS)   R(toR)   L(turning R to RCF)   R
tap step heelbt: step: 5s.crmp.rl.chge.turn: tap step heelbt:
& a   1   2   a 3 & a 4   & a   5

Trav. bkds to LCB

 L   R   L   R   L   R   L   R   L   R
Step: scuffle: step: scuffle: step: scuffle ball beat: toe tap: *(miss):* heelbt: step: scuffle:
1   & a   2   & a   3   & a   4   &   *(5)*   a   1 & a

 L   R   L   R L
Step: scuffle ball-beat: 3s.shuffle: heelbt: step:
2   & a   3   a 4 &   a   5

Face RS and travel to just beyond centre

      R   L   R   L   L R L   R
Single waltz clog: double waltz clog: tap spring heelbt: shuffle bll.chge: chug: chug:
 1 a 2 a 3   & a 4 & a 5   & a   1   a 2 a 3 4   5

Diagonally L to centre

 L R(turn L):   R L   R(face front) R(fwd)   R
Step: toe tap: *(miss):* bll.chge: 4s.crmp.rl: stamp: *(miss):* clp.pll.bk.chge. *(miss):*
1   <u>&</u>   *(2)*   a 3   nna4   <u>&</u>   *(5)*   nna1   *(2)*

 R   L (ft.tog)
bll.chge: *slide RF to RS and bend L knee:*
a 3   4 5

265 Step into Seven, an excerpt

Music: 'Cut 7' from *Spice Up Your Tap*
Tempo: = 146

First Four Bars

Travel from LCB to RCF
The first two ball changes should be similar to a gallop feeling travelling to RCF.

 L R   L   R(turn to R optional)   L   R   L
Bll.chge: bll.chge(flt): *(miss):*   spring-heel: step heelbt: tap step *(miss):* heelbt
1   +   2   +   *(3)*   4   +   5   + 6 + *(7)*   +

Face RCF

	R	L		L	R	L	R		L	R	L
Tap-step	heelbt:	scuff:	*(miss):*	(bk)brush:	hop:	step:	pu spring:	step:	pll.bk:	heelbt
1	+	2	±	*(3)*	+	4	+	5	+	6	nna7	+

Face front and travel to RS

	R	R	R	L(fwd)	R	L(XfL)		R(toRS)		L(releaseRF.fwd)
Stamp(n):	pll.bk:	step:	brush:	hop:	step heelbt:	tap-step heelbt:		pu step:
1		nna2	+	3	+	4	+	5	+	6		+	7

	R	LtoR		L	R		L	RtoL	R		L
(bk)brush pu.chge:	(fwd)brush pu.1ft:	(bk)brush pu.chge:	3s.ripple:	3s.ripple:
na1		na2			na3		na4	na5

	R		R
rippledown:	4s.crmp.rl:
nna6		nna7

Second Four

	R		L	L	R(toRCF)	L(turn R)		L	R		L
Stamp(n) pu step:	shuffle bll.chge(flt):		brush(side):	*(miss):*	spring step:	tap-step heelbt:
1	+	2	+	3	+	4		+	*(5)*	+	6	+	7	+

Travel backwards to LCB facing LCF

R(toRCF)	L(sdwys)	R	R L(tog)	R(toRCF)	L(sdwys)		R(XbL)		L(sdwys)
Stamp(w):	step:	pu bll.chge:	stamp:	step:	pu step heelbt:	step heelbt
1		+	2	+	3	±	4	+	5	+	6	+

Travelling sideways to RS(bk)

R(fwd)	L	R(fwd)	R	L		R	L	R(toRS)	L(XbR)		R L(XfR)
Stamp(n):	heelbt:	stamp(n)	pu:	hop:	(sd)shuffle:	hop:	step:	pu step heel:	*(miss):*	bll.chge
7		+	1	+	2	+ 3	+	4	+	5	+	*(6)*	+	7

	R	R(fwd)		R	R	R	LtoR	L		L
4s.crmp.rl:	ball dig:	*(miss):*	pll.bk:	pllbk:	snatch pu.chge:	rippledown:	step:
nna1	±	*(2)*	nna3	nna4		na5		nna6	7

Third Four

Travel sideways to R

	R (tog)			R	L	R	L
4s.crmp.rl:	(double travel) ball beat:	ball beat:	heelbt:	heelbt:
nna1			+	2	+	3

		R				L(tog)
(single travel) ball beat	heelbt	ball beat	heelbt	ball beat:	step heelbt:
	+	4	+	5	+	6	7

R(XfL) L(toLS)   R   R   L   R   L R R L   L   R
Stamp(w):   step   pu bll.chge: stamp(w): step pu bll.chge heelbt: (fwd)brush
  1   +   2 + 3   ±   4 + 5 +   6   7

R (tog)   R   L   R   L
4s.crmp.rl: (double travel) ball beat: ball beat: heelbt: heelbt:
  nna1   +   2   +   3

                        R   L
(single travel) ball beat heelbt ball beat heelbt ball beat: step heelbt:
              +   4   +   5   +   6 7

With back to audience turning R and travel to LS
        R   L   R   L   R
Step heelbt: step heelbt: *(miss)*: step heelbt: step heelbt: *(miss)*: step:
  1   +   2   +   *(3)*   4   +   5   +   *(6)*   7

Fourth Four
  L   R   L   R(turn to R optional)   L   R   L
Bll.chge: bll.chge(flt):   *(miss)*:   spring heel: step heelbt: tap step *(miss)*: heelbt
  1   +   2   +   *(3)*   4   +   5   +   6 + *(7)*   +

        R   L   L   R   L   R   L   R   L
Tap step heelbt: scuff: *(miss)*: (bk)brush: hop: step: pu spring: step: pll.bk: heelbt
  1   +   2   ±   *(3)*   +   4   +   5   +   6   nna7   +

Face front and travel to RS
  R   R   R(fwd) L   R   L(XfL)   R   L
Stamp(n): pll.bk: step: brush: hop: step heelbt: tap step heelbt: pu step:
  1   nna2   +   3   +   4   +   5   +   6   + 7

  L   R   L   L   R   R   R   R
Heelbt flam(outs): press crmp.rl: *(miss)*: heelbt: flam(ins): 4s.crmp.rl: stamp: chug:
  n   n1   nna2   *(3)*   n   n4   n n a 5   6   7

266 Soft shoe dance, an excerpt
Music: Duke Ellington CD.20a, track 16, *I let a Song Go Out of my Heart*.
Tempo: 108.

Introduction
Four bars. Wait for seven counts.

        L   R   L   R
Tap-step bll.chge:(light)stamp(n) pu step:(light)stamp(n):(slideL.bk.w) heelbt heelbt
  a   8 a 1   a   2 a   3   a   4

```
        L  R     L     R
(miss): bll.chge: tap step: step:
 (5)    a  6     a  7   8
```

Section A (eight bars)
Single essence twice   **Double essence** once
```
L and R    a 1 & a 2 a 3 & a 4         LF    a 5 & a 6 & a 7 & a 8
```

Bambalina and break
```
       R                 L        R   L  R   L    R    L   R  L  R    L
Bambalina (with hop) pu spring: shuffle: hop: step: brush: hop: step: step: bll.chge: step:
  a1&a2                & a     3 &   a   4   &    a    5    6  a 7    8
```

Virginia essence (173)
```
Commencing R and then L    a 1 & a 2 a 3 & a 4
Break
       R      L  R      L  R      R          L      R        L
Heel dig(w): step scuffle: step scuffle: ball beat: toe tap: heelbt: toe tap:
   a       5    &a   6    &a     7        &     a     8
```

```
   R    L      R              R  L    R            L
Heelbt:  step into toe-beat drag turn: (miss): bll.chge:  7s.riff:   5s.riff:
   a    1      &              (2 3)  a 4   &a5&a6&    a7&a8
```

Section B (eight bars)
Travel sideways to RCF
Grapevine step twice   **Break (with grapevine)**
```
Commence hop L then R  a 1 & a 2 a 3 & a 4    Commence hop L:   a 5 & a 6 a 7 a 8
```

```
Break
  L    R(toRCF)       R     L     R     L    R    L    R(XbL)
stomp:   scuff:   (bk)brush: hop: (sd)shuffle: hop: toe tap: 2s.hop:  step
  a      1         a     2     &a   3   &    n    n     a
```

```
L(turn in out – single travel to LS)
  Ball dig:       heelbt: ball beat:
    4                &       a
```

```
R(XbL)       L(turning in and out – single travel)       R(toRS)
step heelbt:   ball-dig heelbt: ball-beat heelbt ball-beat:  step heelbt:
  5    a        6        &      a        7      &       a   8
```

```
Face RS and travel backwards to LS
```
Back essence   **Link** R(XbL)   **Back essence**
```
Commence L:  a 1 a 2      (bk)brush step      Commence L:   a 4 a 5
                             a     3
```

Link (facing front)

R(toRS)   *(drag L to R)*

Stamp: *(miss):*

   &   *(6 7 8)*

Alternative break (177)   a1&a2&a3&a4&a5 6 7 a8

Section C (eight bars)

Travelling sideways in a circle from LCF across front of stage and finish LCB

R   L(w.turn to R)   R   L(fwd) R(toRS) L   R   L(XbR)

Step: ball dig(w): *(miss):* tap step heelbt: stamp: step   pu: hop: step:

1   &   *(2)* & a   3   a   4   & a   5

R R L   R(fwd) L(XbL)   R

Shuffle bll.chge: tap step: toe beat: heelbt:

a 6 & a   7 &   a   8

L   R   R   L L R   L   R   L

Stamp: scuff(flt): (bk)brush step: pu bll.chge: pu: hop: step:

a   1   a   2   & a   3   & a   4

R R L   R(bk) L   R   L   R   L

shuffle bll.chge(flt): step: pu: hop: step: (str)shuffle: hop:

& a 5 &   a   6 & a   7 &   a

Travel sideways to RCF

R R L   R   L(XbL) R R L

Shuffle bll.chge: (fwd)tap heel-dig(w): pu step: pu bll.chge:

8 & a   1   a   2   a   3   & a   4

R   L(XbL) R R L   R(extend L bhd)

(fwd)tap heel-dig(w): pu step: pu bll.chge: drop(flt):   *(miss):*

a   5   a   6   & a 7   a   *(8)*

Break (176)

Commence L: a 1 & a 2 & a 3 & a 4 & a 5 a 6 a 7 & a 8

Section D (eight bars)
Toe-heel clip combination (180)

Commence L: 1 a 2 a 3 & a 4 & a 5 & a 6 a 7 & a 8

Repeat first half commencing R: 1 a 2 a 3 & a 4

Continue with link using heel-toe-clip (37) and toe-heel.clip.trav (38)

Travel to RS

L to R   R   L(XfR)   R to L   L   R(toRS)

Heel-toe-clip(37): ball beat: step: toe-heel-clip.trav(38): heelbt: step:

&   a   5   &   a   6

L to R   R L(XfR)   R to L   L R(toRS)
Heel-toe-clip(37): ball beat: step: toe-heel-clip.trav(38): heelbt: stamp:
 &   a   7   &   a <u>8</u>

       L   R   R
(miss): ball dig(w): *(miss)*: ball dig(n): *(miss)*: ball dig(w): *(miss)*:
 (1)   a   *(2)* a   *(3)* a   *(4)*

       L   R   L   R
(sd)shuffle step heelbt: stamp(n) pu step: shuffle step: stamp(w):
 a 5 & a <u>6</u> & a 7 & a   <u>8</u>

Alternative break (178)
Commence L: a 1 & a 2 & a 3 n & a 4 & a 5 6 7 & a 8 (using the alternative ending)

N.B. On the counts '6, 7' make a complete turn to the right (a quarter on '6' and three quarters on '7').

Alternative end:
 R L R
Chug chug chug
 &   a   8

267 Two for Tap
Music: CD.17 *Sleepless In Seattle*; track 8, *A Wink and a Smile*.
Tempo: Crotchet = 113
Cannon and counter rhythm: This excerpt from a sequence is arranged for two dancers dancing complementary rhythms. Part of it is arranged in counter rhythm, with different rhythms being performed simultaneously; part of it is arranged in cannon – one dancer commencing two or four beats ahead of the other; part of it is arranged in unison.

Introduction (in unison)
Wait seven counts.
 R L R   L   R   L R
Bll.chge: step: shuffle: hop: step: step:
 a 8 1   a 2 a   3 4

First Eight Bars
Dancer 1
L(toLS) R R L   R   L L R L   R   L L R
Tap step pu bll.chge: tap step heelbt: pu bll.chge: spring: tap-heel-ball: (sd)shuffle bll.chge:
 a 1 & a 2 & a 3 & a 4 n a 5 a   6 & a 7
Dancer 2
L(toR) R L R   R R L R L L R
Touch: heelbt: step: touch: *(miss):* step: heelbt: scuff(hl): heelbt: step: heelbt: scuff(hl)
 1   a 2 a *(3)* 4 a   5   a 6 a 7

Dancer 1

L	R	LtoR	L(bR)	R	L	R	LtoR	L
Drop(flt):	shuffle	pu.chge:	step:	step	heelbt:	drop(flt):	shuffle:	pu.chge: step:
8	nn	n a	1	a	2	3	nn	n a	4

Dancer 2

L	R	R	L	R		L		R(XbL)
heelbt:	step:	heelbt:	heelbt:	stamp(n):	*(miss):*	heelbt(dragging RF bk):		step:
a	8	a	1	&	*(2)*	3		4

Dancer 1

	RL(XfR)	R		L		R	L		R
(miss):	bll.chge:	step	heelbt:	toe tap:	*(miss):*	heelbt:	step	heelbt:	*(miss):* shuffle
(5)	a 6	a	7	<u>&</u>	*(8)*	a	1	<u>&</u>	*(2)*	a 3

Dancer 2

L	R	L(XbR)	R(toRS)	L	R	L(XbR)	R	L R
stamp(w):	stamp(w):	step:	step:	stamp(w):	stamp(w):	step:	step:	bll.chge:
a	5	6	7	a	8	1	2	a 3

Dancer 1

R	L	R	RL	R	L	L R	R	L	R	L	R
bll.chge:	shuffle:	bll.chge:	step:	shuffle	bll.chge	heelbt	chug:	*(miss):*	chug	chug	stamp(n):
a 4	a 5	&	a 6	a 7	& a	8	1	(2)	a	3	<u>&</u>

Dancer 2

L	R	L		L	R	R(toL)	R	L(XbR)
Step:	step:	step:	*(miss):*	heelbt:	stamp(n):	drag:	chug:	step:
4	5	6	*(7)*	a	8	1	2	3

Dancer 1

	L(XfR)		R
(miss):	step:		7s.hopping riff:
(4)	5		6 & a 7 & a 8

Dancer 2

R	L(XbL)	L	R		R	R
chug:	step:	heelbt:	stamp(w):	*(miss):*	chug:	chug:
4	5	6	&	*(7)*	a	8

Section B

Dancer 1

L	R	L	R(XbL)	R	L	R	L		L	R	L	R	L R
Spring:	shuffle:	hop:	step	hop	shuffle:	hop:	step:	*(miss):*	hop	shuffle	hop	step:	bll.chge:
a	1&	a	2	a	3 &	a	4	(5)	a	6 &	a	7	a 8

Dancer 2

L R	L R	L	R	L	R(XbL)	R	L	R	L		L	R
Bll.chge:	bll.chge:	spring:	shuffle:	hop:	step	hop	shuffle:	hop:	step:	*(miss):*	hop	shuffle
a 1	a 2	a	3 &	a	4	a	5 &	a	6	*(7)*	a	8 &

Dancer 1
```
L    R      L      R           R    R(toe.drag.L.andextendfwd)        L
Bll.chge: step heelbt: toe beat: (miss): step:  chug  chug  chug          (bk)tap step:
a    1      a      2        &    (3)     4     5     6     7              a    8
```
Dancer 2
```
L  R L R    L R         L      R         R    R(toe drag.L.and extend) L
hop step: bll.chge: bll.chge: step heelbt: toe-beat: (miss): step  chug:      (bk)tap step:
a    1  a 2    a    3    a    4      &    (5)    6    7              a    8
```

Travelling backwards

Dancer 1
```
R    L    R L      R           L R    L R         L
Bll.chge: bll.chge: Bambalina(w.hop):  bll.chge:  bll.chge:  Bambalina(w.hop):
a    1    a    2    a 3 & a 4          a    5     a    6     a 7 & a 8
```
Dancer 2
```
      R         L R L R         L         R L    R L
Bambalina(w.hop):  bll.chge:  bll.chge:  Bambalina(w.hop): bll.chge:  bll.chge:
a   1 & a   2    a    3    a    4    a 5 & a 6         a    7    a    8
```

Dancer 1
```
  R              L                    L R   L           R
Flap:   (miss):  shuffle crmp.rl(5s.): (miss):  step:  bll.chge:  standing crmp.rl:
a1       (2)     a 3 & a 4            (5)     6    a    7         a 8 & a 1
```
Dancer 2
```
      R              L            L R   L         R
(miss):  flap:   (miss) :  shuffle crmp.rl:  bll.chge: step:  standing crmp.rl:
(1)      a 2      (3)      a 4 & a 5       a    6    7        a 8 & a 1
```

Section C
Dancer 1
```
       L    R    L    R    L    R    L
(miss):  pu step: pu step: flap: chug: chug: walk: walk:
(2)      a    3  a    4  a    5  a    6    7    8
```
Dancer 2
```
R(releaseLfwd)        L              R    L              R         L
Stomp:       (bk)brush spring:  (sd)shuffle step:  pu spring:  shuffle spring: step heelbt:
2                a    3          &a   4    a    5    a6        a    7    a
```

Dancer 1
```
  L    R      L      R      L      R      L    R         L R  L    L
Heelbt: step heelbt: scuff(hl): heelbt: step heelbt: scuff(hl): heelbt: step (miss): bll.chge: step:
a    1    a    2    a    3    a    4    a    5    (6)    a 7    8
```
Dancer 2
```
R    L      R        L    L(finish RF front)  R    R    R L(ft.apart)
Step heelbt: spring: shuffle spring: shuffle single waltz:       pll.bk: pll.bk: bll.chge
8    a    1    & a   2      & a   3 a 4 a 5       nna6  nna7  a 8
```

In Unison

	R	L	R	L	tog.	tog.	
(bk)essence:	(bk)tap step:	(bk)essence:	(bk)tap step *(miss)*:	jump:	chug:	*(miss)*:
a 1 a 2	a 3	a 4 a 5	a 6 *(7)*	8	<u>1</u>	*(2 3 4)*

No. One RF.   No. Two LF

Step:	Cahito three times:	(extra bar)	Bambalina twice:
5	&a6&a7&a8		a1&a2 a3&a4

Section D
Dancer 1

	R		L	R	R L	
stamp(n)	pu step heelbt:	shuffle step:	stamp(n) pu bll.chge(flt):			
<u>a</u>	1 & a	2 & a	<u>3</u> & a <u>4</u>			

Dancer 2

L		R		L	R	R L
Step	stamp(n) pu step heelbt:	shuffle step:	stamp(n) pu bll.chge(flt):			
1	<u>&</u> a 2	& a 3	& <u>a</u> 4 & <u>a</u>			

Dancer 1

	R		L	R	R L	R
Stamp(n)	pu step heelbt:	shuffle step:	stamp(n) pu bll.chge(flt):	stamp(n)		
<u>a</u>	5 & a	6 & a	<u>7</u> & a <u>8</u>	1		

Dancer 2

R		L		R	L	L R
Step heelbt:	stamp(n) pu step heelbt:	shuffle step:	stamp(n) pu bll.chge(flt):			
5 &	<u>a</u> 6 & a	7 & a	<u>8</u> & a <u>1</u>			

Dancer 1

	R		L	R	R L	
Crmp.rl time-step(dbl):	Crmp.rl time-step(dbl trpl):	stomp:	*(miss):* hop: step:			
a 2 a 3 a 4 & a 5	a 6 & a 7 & a 8 & a 1	<u>&</u>	*(2, 3)* a 4			

Dancer 2

R		L	R	R	L R	
Crmp.rl time-step(dbl):	crmp.rl time-step(dbl.trpl):	pll.bk:	pll.bk:	hop: step		
a 2 a 3 a 4 & a 5	a 6 & a 7 & a 8 & a 1	nna2	nna3	a 4		

(Both feet on ground for single and double travel – turning feet in and out alternately)

Dancer 1

R(in)	R(turned out in out)	L(out)	R(in)	L(in)	R(out)	R(in. out)		L
Stamp(w) ball-bt heelbt ball-bt:	heelbt:	heelbt: ball-bt:	ball-bt:	heelbt ball-bt:	tap step heelbt:			
8	1	2	3	a 4	a 5	6	7 a 8 &	

Dancer 2

R(in)	R(turned out in out)	L(out)	R(in)	L(in)	R(out)	R(in. - out - in)
Stamp(w) ball-bt heelbt ball-bt:	heelbt:	heelbt:	ball-bt:	ball-bt	heelbt ball-bt heelbt	
8	1	2	3	a 4	a 5	6 7 8

137

Section E
Dancer 1

R	L	R	L	R	L	R	L	R

Stamp(n) pu: hop: (sd)shuffle: hop: toe tap: 2s.hop: step: pu spring: stamp(n)

 1 & a   2 &   a 3   & a   4   & a   <u>5</u>

Dancer 2

 L   L   R L   R L R

Touch   step: stamp(n) pu: hop: (sd)shuffle: hop: toe tap:

 1   2   3   & a   4 &   a 5

Dancer 1

R	L	R	L	R

pu step heelbt: stamp(n) pu spring: (sd)shuffle spring: (sd)shuffle spring: step:

& a 6   <u>&</u>   a 7   & a   8   & a 1   2

Dancer 2

 L R L   R   L   R

2s.hop: step: pu spring: stamp(n) pu step heelbt: stamp(n) pu spring: (sd)shuffle spring:

& a 6 & a   <u>7</u>   & a 8   <u>&</u>   a 1   & a   2

Dancer 1

L(toLS)	R	L	R(XbL)	L(toLS)	R(toRS)	L(bsdR)

step: (sd)shuffle: hop: step heelbt: step heelbt: *(miss)*: step heelbt: step heelbt:

 3   n &   a 4 &   a 5   *(6)*   a 7   a 8

Dancer 2

 L   R L(toLS)   R   L   R(bL)   L(toLS)

(sd)shuffle spring: step: step: (sd)shuffle: hop: step heelbt: step heelbt: *(miss)*:

 & a 3   4   5   n &   a 6 &   a 7   *(8)*

Dancer 1

R	R		L	R	L	R (turning to the R)	L R L R

rev.crmp.rl: step: *(miss)*:   step: bll.chge: step: bll.chge: bll.chge

 a 1& a   2   *(3)*   4   a 5   6   a 7   a 8

Dancer 2

 R(toRS)   L(bsdR)   R   R   L R (turning R) L R

step heelbt: step heelbt: rev.crmp.rl: step: *(miss)*: bll.chge: bll.chge: bll.chge:

 a 1   a 2   a 3& a   4   *(5)*   a 6   a 7   a 8

In Unison

 L   R   L   R

(miss): step stomp: *(miss)*: back essence: step stomp: *(miss)*: (str)tap:

 (1)   2 <u>&</u>   *(3)*   a 4 a 5   6 <u>&</u>   *(7)*   8

Section F
Dancer 1

L	R	L	R	L	R	L	R	R L L

Heelbt:shuffle:heelbt: toe tap: heelbt: 6s.riff   heel-dig pu step heelbt: shuffle bll.chge heelbt:

 a   1 &   a   2   a 3&a4&a 5   & a 6   a 7 & a 8

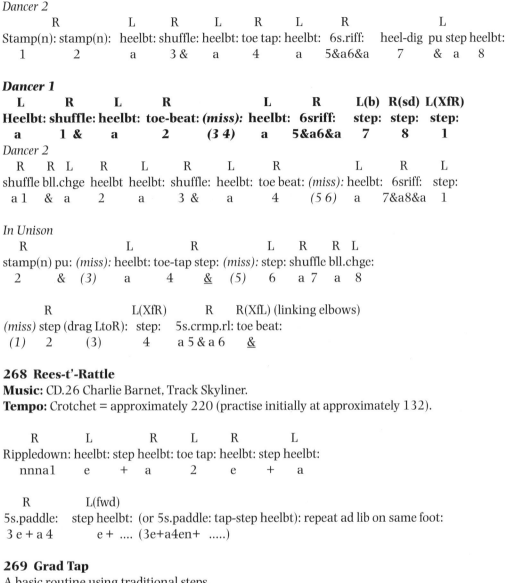

Dancer 2

R		L	R	L	R	L	R		L
Stamp(n):	stamp(n):	heelbt:	shuffle:	heelbt:	toe tap:	heelbt:	6s.riff:	heel-dig	pu step heelbt:
1	2	a	3 &	a	4	a	5&a6&a	7	& a 8

Dancer 1

L	R	L	R		L	R	L(b)	R(sd)	L(XfR)
Heelbt:	**shuffle:**	**heelbt:**	**toe-beat:**	*(miss):*	**heelbt:**	**6sriff:**	**step:**	**step:**	**step:**
a	**1 &**	**a**	**2**	**(3 4)**	**a**	**5&a6&a**	**7**	**8**	**1**

Dancer 2

R	R	L	R	L	R	L	R		L	R	L
shuffle	bll.chge	heelbt	heelbt:	shuffle:	heelbt:	toe beat:	*(miss):*	heelbt:	6sriff:	step:
a 1	&	a	2	a	3 &	a	4	(5 6)	a	7&a8&a	1

In Unison

R		L	R		L	R	R L
stamp(n) pu:	*(miss):*	heelbt:	toe-tap step:	*(miss):*	step:	shuffle bll.chge:
2	& (3)	a	4	<u>&</u> (5)	6	a 7 a 8

	R	L(XfR)	R	R(XfL) (linking elbows)
(miss) step (drag LtoR):	step:	5s.crmp.rl:	toe beat:
(1) 2	*(3)*	4	a 5 & a 6	<u>&</u>

268 Rees-t'-Rattle

Music: CD.26 Charlie Barnet, Track Skyliner.
Tempo: Crotchet = approximately 220 (practise initially at approximately 132).

R	L	R	L	R	L
Rippledown:	heelbt:	step heelbt:	toe tap:	heelbt:	step heelbt:
nnna1	e	+ a	2	e	+ a

R	L(fwd)
5s.paddle:	step heelbt: (or 5s.paddle: tap-step heelbt): repeat ad lib on same foot:
3 e + a 4	e + ... (3e+a4en+ .....)

269 Grad Tap

A basic routine using traditional steps.
Music: CD.20c, *Dancers In Love* (Track 6), Duke Ellington, *Essential Collection, Year 1956–62.*
Tempo: Crotchet = approximately 200.
Vocabulary: American roll: Bambalina: pu or buck time-step: Buffalo: Cahito: Chicago roll: combination Maxi-ford: falling off the log: Irish: Manhattan time-step variation: over the top: rattle: rattle: dble.toe-tap.prog.rattle: riff (6s): roll time-step: running flaps: shuffle off to Buffalo: Cubanola: stamp scuff time-step.

Introduction

Wait

Section A

American roll one-and-a-half times commence LF: Sh-off-to-Buffalo twice L:
8na1+2+3+4+5+6+7 8na1+2+3   +4&a5+6&a7

Irish once L: Sh-off-to-Buffalo once R: Irish twice R L: Rattle R:
 +8+1   +2&a3   +4+5+6+7   +8+1+2+3+4+5+6+7

Section B

```
          R                    R(toRS)        R  L      R(toRS)      L(toLS)
Dbl.toe-tap.prog.rattle:         scuff:   (miss): bll.chge: step heelbt: step heelbt:
+8+1+2+3+4+5+6+7na8    1       (2 3)   + 4       5        6        7        8
```

```
    R(toRS)        L        R(ft tog)       L
Tap-step heelbt: heelbt: pu step heelbt: heelbt:
 +    1    +      2    +   3    +    4
```

```
    R(toRS)        L        R  L(Rlift.b) R(toLCF)            L                    L
Tap-step heelbt: heelbt: pu:   heelbt:   6s.riff:   toe-beat-drag (drag): stamp(w) stomp:
 +    5    +      6    +     7    +8+1+2       3        (4 5)       6              7
```

Section C

Travel to LS

```
       L                L(bR)  R  L(XfR)          R        L     R     L
fall off the log twice: toe tap: hop: toe tap: (miss) over the top: toe tap: hop: toe tap:
8&a1 2 3 4&a5 6 7     8      1    +     (2)       +         3     +     4
```

```
     L         R         L    R L         R       LRLR(bkds.twds RCB)
Tap spring: tap spring: tap step: bll.chge: clap: step:   Cahito(draw back) four times:
 +     5     +   6       +   7   +   8     +   1      + 2 + 3 + 4 + 5 + 6 + 7
```

```
   L      R         L   R   L   L          L
step: Bambalina:  step: step: chug chug (miss): chug:
 8    a 1 & a 2     3    4    5    6     (7)     8
```

Section D

Starting with stamp on count '1' (instead of 8)

```
              R     L           R      L
pu (or buck) double t/s twice:    stamp(w): stamp(w):
1 + 2 + 3 + 4 + 5 + 6 + 7 + 8 +    1         +
```

```
             R                 R      L      R      L
pu (or buck) double t/s twice:    stamp(w): stamp(w): stamp(w): stamp(w):
2 + 3 + 4 + 5 + 6 + 7 + 8 + 1 +   2         +         3         +
```

```
   R           L         R      R        L   R
pu double t/s:   pu triple t/s:   stamp(n): Bambalina: pu: heelbt
4 + 5 + 6 + 7 +  8+1&a2+3+     4         + 5 &a 6    +   7
```

140

Section E

	L		R	R L		R
	Combn M/F:		break to combn M/F:	Chicago roll:		break to Chicago roll:
	8&a1+2+3+4+5+6+7		81 a2na3 4 a5 na6 7	+8+1+2+3+4+5+6+7		+8+1+2(3)+4+5(6)+7

Section F

Move to LCF, then circle, turning R, to LCB – then diagonally to RCF.

L(toLS)	R(XfL)	L(toLS)	R(toR)	R	L(XfR)	L	R	L	R(turn)
Step:	step:	step heelbt:	4s.crmp.rl:	ball-dig:	step	*(miss)*:	heelbt:	step:	step:	step:
8	1	2	3	4nn5	6	7	*(8)*	a	1	2	3

L	R	L(XfR)	L	R	L(turn)	R	L	R
crmp.rl-chge.turn:	ball-dig:	step	*(miss)*:	heelbt:	step:	step:	step:	crmp.rl-chge.turn:	step
4 n a 5	6	7	*(8)*	a	1	2	3	4 n a 5	6

Sideways to RCF

R		L(XfR)	R(to side)		L to R	R		L	R
heelbt:	*(miss)*:	step heel:	step heelbt:	clip-bll.chge:	heelbt:	heelbt:	step:	*(miss)*:
7	*(8)*	a	1	2	3	4	n	a	5	6	7	*(8)*

Section G

L	R(turnR)	L(XfR)	R	L	R	R		L	R	L	R
bll.chge:		step heelbt:	shower-flap	step	chug	*(miss)*:	chug:	chug:	chug:	stamp(n):
a	1	2	3	4 n a 5	6	7	*(8)*	a	1	2	3

L	R	R	LR(turn)	L(fwd)	R	L
Press crmp.rl:	stamp(n):	stamp(w):	*(miss)*:	bll.chge:	step heelbt:	rippledown:	heelbt:
4 n a 5	6	7	*(8)*	a	1	2	3	4 n a 5	6

R(sdwys)		LR(turn)	L(fwd)		R
stamp(w):	*(miss)*:	bll.chge:	step heelbt:	rippledown:	*(miss)*:
7	*(8)*	a	1	2	3	4 n a 5	(6 7)

Section H
Facing front

Cubanola (travelling time-step) three times (sgl. dbl and trpl and break)

8+1+2+3+4 5 6+7+ 8+1+2+3+4 5+6+7+ 8+1+2+3+4 5&a6+7+ 8+1+2+3+4+5+6+7

Section J

Face LCF and travel back twds RCB

	R(bk)	L(bk)	R	R(bk)		L(fwd)		R		R(fwd)
(miss):	step:	step:	pll.bk:	step:	*(miss)*:	step heelbt:	rippledown:	step:	*(miss)*:
(8 1)	2	3	4na5	6	*(7 8 1)*	2	3	4 n a 5	6	*(7 8)*

141

Sideways to RCB

L(bR)	R(sd)	L(XfR)	R	R	L(fwd)		L	R	L(bk)
Step:	step:	step:	rev.crmp.rl:	step:	step	*(miss)*:	heelbt:	step:	step:
1	2	3	4 n a 5	6	7	*(8)*	1	2	3

	R		R	
Tip-top pull back (or pll.bk):		step:	*(miss)*:	
	4 n a 5		6	*(7)*

Section K

	L		L						L	
Manhattan time-step variation (with chugs) twice: commencing LF: chug *(miss)*:										

+8+1+2+3+4+5+6+7+8+1+2+3+4+5+6+7   ±

R	L	R	L		R	L	R	L		R		R	
Chug:	chug:	chug:	chug:*(miss)*		chug:	chug:	chug:	chug:*(miss)*		stamp(n):*(miss)*		stamp(n):*(miss)*	
1	2	3	±	*(4)*	5	6	7	±	*(8)*	1	*(2)*	3	*(4)*

Section L

Cutaway (159) with or without 'over the top'.

L	R(XfL)	L(RLstretched behind)	R(w.LXfR)		R(overL)		
Spring:	toe tap	stomp:	*(miss)*	spring:	over-the-top:	*(miss)*:	
1	2	3	*(4)*	5	*(6)*	7	*(8)*

Repeat cutaway with 'over the top' 1 2 3 *(4)* 5 *(6)* 7 *(8)*

R(Lstretched behind)		L	R(bL)	R	(LXfR)	R(overL)	L(bR)
Stomp:		spring:	toe tap:	drop:	toe tap:	over the top:	toe tap
1		2	3	4	5	*(6)* 7	8

Section M

L		R	R			R(turn in	out	in)
Step:	*(miss)*:	pll.bk:	stamp(w):	*(miss)*:	clip: clip:	ball-beat	ball-beat	ball-beat:
1	*(2)*	nna3	4	*(5)*	6 7	8	1	2

	L		R	L(bR)	R	L(XfR)	L	L	
Stamp chug:		stamp chug:		step:	paddle:	step:	heel-tap:	heelbt:	*(miss)*
3		4		5	6	7	8 + 1 +	2 3	+ *(4)*

Stamp scuff time-step once with half the break (220)

R	L	R(circleLout)		L	R	L	L R	L R	
Stamp:	scuff:	stomp:	(bk)brush step:	pu step:	shuffle	bll.chge(flt):	bll.chge(flt):		
1	2	3	+ 4	+ 5	+ 6	+ 7	+ 8		

	L(to LS)		R(XfL)		L		L(XfR)	L(XfL)	
Tap-step heelbt:		tap-step heelbt:		(fwd)brush:		(bk)brush:	step heelbt:		
+ 1	2	+ 3	4	5		6	7	8	

Grad tap, the alternative position in the penultimate bar: step RF and join feet tog. – arms reaching up. (The original position 'step on to RF with LF at R knee, arms lifted' is shown on front cover.)

Step on to RF and balance with LF at R knee arms lifted L (or step with ft tog. on rise – arms reaching up) 1–4

Drop sideways on to LF arms lifted to R, eye line down to left. 5 (6 7 8)

Transfer weight on to RF, drop arms (1) and turn head slowly to front (within music).

CONTRIBUTIONS FROM FRIENDS

270 Joy Jingle

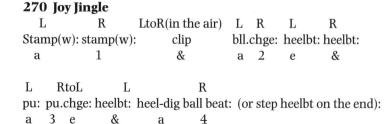

L	R	LtoR(in the air)	L	R	L	R
Stamp(w):	stamp(w):	clip	bll.chge:		heelbt:	heelbt:
a	1	&	a	2	e	&

L	RtoL	L	R		
pu:	pu.chge:	heelbt:	heel-dig ball beat:	(or step heelbt on the end):	
a	3	e	&	a	4

271 Victor Leopold's cutaway, contributed by Daphne Peterson
(Shuffle pick-up change with 'cutaway')

	R	L to R	L(XfR)	R (releasing LL behind)		
(bk)shuffle	pu.chge:	toe tap:	hop (on whole foot):	repeat LF:	repeat RF
n n	a 1	+	2	nnna3 + 4	nnna5 + 6

L	R(XfL)	L	R(XbL)
Drop:	toe tap:	hop:	toe tap:
+	7	+	8

272 Jim Taylor's '1 2 3 4' accented paddle and roll
Tempo: = 100 to 110
Vocabulary: Paddle and roll: single, double and triple stamps.

(Moving to RS)

R to R	L(XbR)	R	L	R	R	L	R	L
Stamp(w):(bk)flap.heelbt:	paddle:paddle:stamp(n):stamp(w):(bk)flap	heelbt:paddle:paddle:
1	( )	+ a	2	e+a3	e+a4	+	5	( )	+ a	6	e+a7	e+a8

R	R	R	L(XbR)	R	L	L	L	L
Stamp(n):stamp(n):stamp(w):(bk)flap	heelbt:paddle:stamp(n):stamp(n):stamp(n):stamp(n):
+	1	+	2 e	+ a 3 e+	4	+	5	+

	R(XfL)			R	L	R	L
(miss):	shuffle step:	(heel-ball turn)	heelbt:	heelbt:	ball beat:	ball beat:
(6)	+ a 7		e	+	a	8

273 David Needham's Tap Break
A step from the choreography of the tap dance 'Who's That Woman?' in the
2002 London production *The Follies.*

Both feet simultaneously	L	RtoL	R(XfL)
Chug forward :	pu:	pu.chge:	toe-tap
1	2	& a	3

R(fwd.toRCF)	L	RtoL	R	L	R	L
Stamp(w):	shuffle:	pu.chge:	step:	tap step:	bll.chge (to face LS – knees bent)
4	a 5	& a	6	a 7	a 8

R	L	R	L	RtoL	R(XbL)
(fwd)brush:	hop:	(bk)brush drop(flt):	shuffle:	pu.chge:	toe tap:
a	1	a 2	a 3	& a	4

Turn and travelling to RCF

R	L	L	R	L

Stamp(w): toe tap: bll.chge: stamp(w): (Finish LF XfR on bent knees)

<u>5</u>   6   a   7   <u>8</u>

Eddie Brown

Eddie's classes were challenging and stimulating, and his creative genius never failed to produce new and complex sequences. These were always carefully analysed with endless patience coupled with a sense of fun. The following are three of the time-step sequences he taught. The first he called a 'rolling wing time-step with a unique break' – and then added: '...and it's the break that makes the step – it makes that step, do you see what I mean?' There is, in fact, no wing contained in the time-step. His many comments, such as 'Answer me!' or 'One .... two .... you know what to do ...' are as memorable as his steps. Eddie also created his own 'B.S. Chorus', which is still danced by his many fans in various parts of the world.

274 Rolling wing time-step with a unique break

L	R	L(toR)	L

4s.ripple: (bk)dbl shuffle: pu.chge heelbt: (bk)dbl shuffle

 nna 1   & a   2 &   nna   3&4

R(toL)	R	L	R	L	R

pu.chge: toe tap: heelbt: (sd)shuffle step: stamp(n) pu step: stamp(n)

 na5   &   n   a 6   &   7   & a   8

Repeat commencing R   Repeat commencing L, but finish stamp(w)

The break

L	R	L	R	R	L	both	R	L

4s.ripple: toe tap: heelbt: shuffle heel-dig(w): heel-dig(w) toe clip: ball-beat ball-beat

 nna1   &   a   2 &   a   3   &   a   4

R	L	R	L	R

Heel-dig pu: heelbt: toe tap: heelbt: 4s.riff:

 &   a   5   &   a   6 & a 7

275 Eddie's riff time-step

R	L(bR)	R	L	L	R	L

4s.riff heelbt: (bk)tap step: shuffle step heelbt: stamp(n): flap: flap: 3s.shuffle:

 a 8 & a 1   a   2   a 3   &   a   <u>4</u>   a 5 a 6   na7

Repeat L and R   a 8 & a 1 a 2 a 3 & a <u>4</u> a 5 a 6 na7. a 8 & a 1 a 2 a 3 & a <u>4</u> a 5 a 6 na7.

Break

L	R	L	R	L	R

4s.riff heelbt: 4s.riff heelbt: (bk)tap step heel: stamp(n) pu step: tap step heelbt heelbt: scuff:

 a 8 & a 1   a 2 & a 3   a   4   &   <u>a</u>   5   &   a   6   &   a   <u>7</u>

276 Shuffle-flap time-step

Close-work rhythm tap. The footwork should be very small, and the whole sequence completed in less than fourteen seconds. The first shuffle, although a side shuffle, is very close to the supporting foot. The flap is taken just at the side of the supporting heel so that the step travels backwards.

```
           R      L      R
(sd)shuffle flap: heelbt: heelbt:  repeat commencing LF:
   1 e + n       a       2        3 e + n a 4
```

```
                          L      R
Repeat commencing RF: paddle: paddle
     5 e + n a 6           e + a 7  e + a 8
```

Repeat the whole commencing with LF: repeat the whole commencing with RF:

Break

This uses the same sequence as the first two counts of the sequence, but it contains two extra heelbts and the rhythm is cross-accented.

```
        L      R      L      R      L
(sd)shuffle flap: heelbt: heelbt: heelbt: heelbt:  repeat R:    repeat L:
   1 e + n      a      2      e      +      na3e+na4  e+na5e+a
```

```
  R      L      R      LtoR      L
Paddle: heelbt: shuffle pu.chge: scuff
6 e + a     7      e +     n      a      8
```

Alternative break

```
        L      R      L      R      L      R           L
(sd)shuffle flap: heelbt: heelbt: paddle: paddle: paddle:  continuous shuffles
   1 e + n      a      2      e + a 3  e + a 4  e + a 5  e + n a 6 e + n a 7
```

```
                L           R
3s.shuffle(sd) step heelbt: scuff:
  e n +      n      a      8
```

From Fred Strickler

277 Tap Dance Concerto (also known as 'Concerto for Tap Dancer and Orchestra')
Score composed by Morton Gould; Fred Strickler's version of choreography.

This eight-bar sequence is from the first movement of the choreography created by Fred Strickler. The 'infinity shape' is Fred's description of the floor pattern (Honi Cole referred to it as a 'cockroach'). A figure of eight is made by the footwork of the 'pick-up step heelbt': it is an outward circle of the foot, and the body follows the movement. The accents, which interpret the musical score, are underlined.

```
      R             L   R     L
Dig  pu  step: dig  pu  step: heelbt: heelbt.
  1   +   2    +   3  +    4        +
```

```
     R       L       R      L
Dig  pu  step:  dig  pu  step:  heelbt:  heelbt.
5   +   6   +   7  +    8       +
```

Infinity shape

```
     R       L         R          L         R
Stamp:  pu  step  heelbt:  dig  pu  step  heelbt:  heelbt:  pu  step  heelbt:
1   e   +   a   2  e   +   a        3   e   +   a
```

facing front   *trav. sideways to R*
```
   L    R    L    R      L         R        L
Paddle:  paddle:  paddle:  stamp:  pu  step  heelbt:  stamp:  pu  step  heelbt:
4e+a 5e+a 6e+a   7   e   +    a        8   e   +    a
```

face front trav. sideways to L
```
   R     L       R          L         R
Paddle:  stamp:  pu  step  heelbt:  stamp:  pu  step  heelbt:
1e+a     2     e  +    a        3     e  +    a
```

face front   sideways to L
```
   L    R     L    R           L    R
Paddle:  paddle:  stamp:  pu  step  heelbt:  paddle:  paddle:
4e+a  5e+a   6     e  +    a     7e+a  8e+a
```

Infinity shape (2)

```
   L       R          L          R          L
Stamp:  pu  step  heelbt:  dig  pu  step  heelbt:  heelbt:  pu  step  heelbt:
1   e   +   a    2  e   +   a       3   e   +   a
```

```
     R         L        R      L    R R R R
Dig  pu  step  heelbt:  heelbt:  pu  step  heelbt:  paddle:  4 heel-digs (lifting foot after each)
4   e   +   a     5    e   +   a    6e+a   7 + 8 +
```

278 B.S. Chorus

Steps and Phrasing of B.S. Chorus

This sequence starts with the 'off-beat' time-step (187). *In the second eight, on count '7' the touch is taken with the knee stretched and the foot towards the open diagonal corner. The last section can be danced as an 'over-the-top' sequence (161) or as a 'cutaway' version. This section would be danced once if using a thirty-two bar piece of music, but could be danced twice if the music includes an extended phrase. The stomp used in the cutaway section is a shunting action (28).

First Eight
Time-Step

```
   R      L   R   L       R
Stamp(n):  hop:  spring:  tap  step:  stamp(w):   repeat 5 times on alternate feet
   8       1    2     a    3      a          456a7a 812a3a 456a7a 812a3a 456a7a
```

147

The B.S. Chorus

In American vaudeville days the B.S. Chorus (so called because it fitted into a standard thirty-two bar tune) was a routine created for chorus girls. They were not expected to perform flash steps or difficult steps, and this basic routine (either tap or non-tap) could be executed well by most chorines. It was very basic, consisting of eight bars of time-step and eight bars of a cross-step, followed by eight bars of buck and wing (simple hops with minimal tapping), the final section being divided equally between 'over the top' and 'through the trenches'. The routine was effective but quick to teach and to perfect. There are many versions of the B.S. Chorus, of which the following is one.

Break

R		L		R		L		R		L	R		L
Stamp(n):	hop:	(sd)shuffle step:	(sd)shuffle step:	(sd)shuffle:	heelbt:	tap step:	tap step:
8	1	e + 2	a 3	a 4a	5	a 6	a 7

Second Eight

R		L		R		L		R		L	R(xFl)		R		L*
Stamp(n):	heelbt:	(bk)shuffle step:	pu step:	(sd)shuffle:	heelbt:	step:	heelbt:	touch
8	1	e + 2	a 3	a 4	a	5	6	7

	R		L		R		L		R	L(XfR)		L		R*
Pause:	heelbt:	(bk)shuffle step:	pu step:	(sd)shuffle:	heelbt:	step:	heelbt:	touch:
(8)	1	e + 2	a 3	a 4	a	5	6	7

	L		R		L		R		L	R(xFl)		R		L(tog)
Pause:	heelbt:	(bk)shuffle step:	pu step:	(sd)shuffle:	heelbt:	step:	heelbt:	step:
(8)	1	e + 2	a 3	a 4	a	5	6	7

R		L		R	R		L	L	R		L	R		L
Stamp(n):	hop:	(sd)shuffle:	step:	(sd)shuffle:	step:	shuffle:	heelbt:	tap step:	tap step:
8	1	+ a 2	+ 3	+ 4 +	5	a 6	a 7

Bridge

	R	L(out to L)		R			L	R	LtoR		L		L
Shuffle step:	(sd)brush:	wing (or hop):	step:	shuffle:	pu.chge:	toe tap:	step:
8 a 1	2	na3	(3)	4	a5	n a	6	7

Repeat with same foot   8 a1 2 3 4 a5 na6 7
Repeat again with same foot   8 a1 2 3 4 a5 na6 7

R		L		R	R	L	L	R		L	R		L
Stamp(n):	hop:	(sd)shuffle:	step:	shuffle:	step:	shuffle:	heelbt:	tap step:	tap step:	Clap:
8	1	e + 2	a 3	a 4a	5	a 6	a 7	8

Last Eight
'Over the top' or cutaway
(Over-the-top version)

R	L(XfR)	R		L	R(XfL)	L	R(bL)
Spring:	toe tap:	over the top	*(pause)*:	spring:	toe tap:	over the top:	toe tap:
1	2	3	(4)	5	6	7	8

R	L(XfR)	R	L	R(XfL)	L	R
Spring:	toe tap:	over the top:	spring:	toe tap:	over the top:	step:
1	2	3	4	5	6	7

Alternative (cutaway version)

R	L(XfR)	R		L	R(XfR)	L	R(bL)
Spring:	toe tap:	stomp(shunt):	*pause*:	spring:	toe tap:	stomp(shunt):	toe tap:
1	+	2	-	3	+	4	+

R	L(XfR)	R	L	R(Xf	L	R
Spring:	toe tap:	stomp(shunt):	spring:	toe tap:	stomp(shunt):	step:
5	+	6	+	7	+	8

Ending
L R L R
4 trenches (160)

		L	L		L	R(in front)
Both						
Jump(fwd on whole foot – ft apart):	pll.bk:	step:	*(pause)*:	hop:	slam.	
5		nna6	+	(7)	+	8

Leonard Reed
279 The Shim Sham Shimmy

The shim sham shimmy has become the national anthem of tap dancers. The latest addition, 'The Revenge', is also included. A teaching video (clearly taught by Rusty Franks) includes comment by Leonard Reed, and a delightful performance by, amongst others, Miriam Nelson and Glen Turnbull.

R	R	R	L	L	L	R	R	R L	R	R	R
Stamp(n):	pu:	step:	stamp(n):	pu:	step:	stamp(n):	pu:	bll.chge:	stamp(n):	pu:	step:
8	a	1	2	a	3	4	a	5 a	6	a	7

Repeat all, commencing LF
8 a 1 2 a 3 4 a 5 a 6 a 7

Repeat all, commencing RF (but finish with ball dig (R beside L) instead of step on count 7)
8 a 1 2 a 3 4 a 5 a 6 a 7

R (diag. fwd)	L(b.R)	LF (bk)	L	R(b.L)		R	L(b.R)	R	L
Stamp	toe tap:	step	heelbt:	step	*(miss)*:	heelbt:	step:	stamp:	stamp
8	1	2	3	a	(4)	a	5	6	7

Cross-over

	R(diag.fwd):	L(bR)	RF (diag. fwd):	L(bR)	R	L		R	L	R
Clap:	stamp:	step	stamp:	step:	step:	scuff(hl):	*(miss)*	heelbt:	step:	step:
8	1	2	3	4	5	a	*(6)*	a	7	8

Repeat the whole, commencing with the stamp LF
1 2 3 4 5 a *(6)* a 7 8

Repeat, commencing with the stamp on RF
1 2 3 4 5 a *(6)* a7 8

L	R		L	R	L	R	L		R	L
Step:	heel-scuff:	*(miss)*:	heelbt:	step:	step:	step:	scuff(hl):	*(miss)*:	heelbt:	step
1	a	*(2)*	a	3	4	5	a	*(6)*	a	7

Tack Annie

R	L	
Stamp(w):	stamp(w):	(feet apart)
a	8	

R	R(bsdL)	R(toR)	L	L(bsdR)	L(toL)	R	R(bsdL)	R(toR)	L	L(bsdR)	R	L(toL)
pu:	ball-dig:	step:	pu:	ball-dig:	step:	pu:	ball-dig:	step:	pu:	step:	stamp:	stamp:
a	1	2	a	3	4	a	5	6	a	7	a	8

Repeat these eight counts (same foot)
a 1 2 a 3 4 a 5 6 a 7 a 8

		L(bsdR)	R(fwd)
Repeat as far as count 6, then:	step:	stamp(w):	
a 1 2 a 3 4 a 5 6	7	8	

L(bR)	L(bk)	L	R(bL)		R	L(bR)	R(fwd)	L(ft.apart)
ball-dig:	step:	heelbt:	step:	*(miss)*:	heelbt:	step:	stamp:	stamp:
1	2	3	a	*(4)*	a	5	6	7

Break

R	L	R	R L	R	L	R	R L
Drop(fl):	step:	(sd)shuffle:	bll.chge:	drop(fl):	step:	(sd)shuffle:	bll.chge:
8	1	a 2	a 3	4	5	a 6	a 7

R	L(bsdR)	L(slightly bk)	L	R(bL)		R:	L(bR):	R(fwd)	L(ft apart)
Stamp:	ball-dig:	step:		heelbt:	step:	*(miss)*:	heelbt:	step:	stamp:	stamp:
8	1	2		3	a	*(4)*	a	5	6	7

Repeat the whole of the break
8 1 a 2 a 3 4 5 a 6 a 7 8 1 2 3 a (4) a 5 6 7

Freeze Chorus

This chorus is exactly the same as the opening shim sham, but with a 'freeze' (pause) for the last two bars. Perform the first six bars as written.

    8 a 1 2 a 3 4 a 5 a 6 a 7   8 a 1 2 a 3 4 a 5 a 6 a 7 8 a 1 2 a 3 4 a 5 a 6 a 7

R(diag.fwd)

Stamp:	*freeze*
8	*(1 2 3 4 5 6 7)*

Cross-over

This is danced as before, with no freeze section.

Tack Annie

Danced as before for the first six bars. Freeze for the seventh and eighth bars, but be ready to start again on count 8 for the next section.

Break

This time the freeze occurs on the third and fourth bars. Be ready to transfer the weight momentarily after the freeze section, ready to use the RF again for the 'drop' on count '8'.

R (fwd)	L		R	R L	R		L		R	R L	R(fwd)
Drop(fl):	step:	(sd)shuffle:	bll.chge:	drop(fl):	step:	(sd)shuffle:	bll.chge:	drop:			
8	1	a 2	a 3	4	5	a 6	a 7	8			

Freeze for seven counts

R	L		R	R L	R		L		R	R L
Drop(fl):	step:	(sd)shuffle:	bll.chge:	drop(fl):	step:	(sd)shuffle:	bll.chge:			
8	1	a 2	a 3	4	5	a 6	a 7			

R	L(bsdR)	L(slightly bk)	L	R(bL)		R	L(bR):	R(fwd)	L(ft apart)
Stamp:	ball-dig:	step:	heelbt:	step:	*(miss)*:	heelbt:	step:	stamp:	stamp:
8	1	2	3	a	*(4)*	a	5	6	7

Shim Sham II

	R		L	R		L	R		L	R
Stamp(n)	pu	step:	repeat:	stamp(n)	pu:	heelbt:	toe-tap:	*(miss)*	heelbt:	step:
8	a	1	2 a 3	4	a	5	a	*(6)*	a	7

Repeat all, commencing LF   Repeat all, commencing RF
8 a 1 2 a 3 4 a 5 a *(6)* a7   8 a 1 2 a 3 4 a 5 a *(6)* a7

	L		R	L		R	L		
Stamp(n)	pu:	heelbt:	toe-tap:	*(miss)*:	heelbt:	step:	Repeat commencing RF:		
8	a	1	a	*(2)*	a	3	4 a 5 a *(6)* a7		

151

Cross-over

The steps on the counts '1 to 5' have a twisting action. The first step on the left is taken with a slight turn to face LS. Then make a small swivel on the LF into the step on to the RF.

L	R	L	R	L	R	L		R	L	
Step:	step:	step:	step:	step:	step:	scuff(hl):	*(miss)*:	heelbt:	step:	rpt twice commencing R & L:
8	1	2	3	4	5	a	*(6)*	a	7	812345a(6)a7 812345a(6)a7

R	L	R		L	R	L	R	L		R	L	R	L(ft.apt)
Step:	step:	scuff(hl):	*(miss)*:	heelbt:	step:	step:	step:	scuff(hl):	*(miss)*:	heelbt:	step:	stamp:	stamp:
8	1	a	*(2)*	a	3	4	5	a	*(6)*	a	7	a	8

Tack Annie

R	R(bsdL)	R(toRS)	L	L(bsdR)	L(toLS)	R	L	R	L	R		L	R	L(ft.apt)
pu:	ball-dig:	step:	pu:	ball-dig:	step:	pu:	heelbt:	step:	pu:	heelbt:	step:	stamp:	stamp:
a	1	2	a	3	4	a	5	a	6	a	7	a	8

Repeat with same foot: Repeat again with same foot:

a1 2a3 4a5a6a7a8   a1 2a3 4a5a6a7a8

R	L	R	L	R		L	R		L	R	L
pu:	heelbt:	step:	pu:	heelbt:	step:	stamp:	stamp:	stamp:	stamp:		
a	1	a	2	a	3	4	5	6	7		

Half Break

	R	L	R	L	R	
Stamp:	step:	shuffle:	heelbt:	step:	Repeat with LF	
8	1	a 2	a	3	4 5 a 6 a 7	

R	L(bR)	L(bk)	L	R(b.L)		R	L(b,R)	R	L
Stamp:	touch:	step:	heelbt:	step:	*(miss)*	heelbt:	step:	stamp:	stamp:
8	1	2	3	a	*(4)*	a	5	6	7

(on counts '3 a (4) a 5' make one turn to own R)

	R	L	R	L	R	
Stamp:	step:	shuffle:	heelbt:	step:	Repeat with LF	
8	1	a 2	a	3	4 5 a 6 a 7	

R	L(b.R)	L(bk)	L	R(b.L)		R	L(b.R)	tog.
Stamp:	touch:	step:	heelbt:	step	*(miss)*:	heelbt:	step:	jump:
8	1	2	3	a	*(6)*	a	5	7

(On counts '3 a (6) a 5' make one turn to own R)

Tag

Both tog		L		L	R	L (carrying RF fwd)		R (with straight leg)
Jump(fwd):	Pull-back:	step:	toe tap:	hop(or heelbt):			flat stamp(in front)(L knee bent):	
1	nna2	a	3	a			4	

Revenge Shim Sham

Leonard Reed created this new version of the shim sham.

First Eight

```
     R      R  L                R          L     L  R            L
Stamp(n)  pu  bll.chge:  stamp(n)  pu  step:  stamp  pu  bll.chge:  stamp  pu  step:
   8      a    1      a      2       a   3      4    a  5   a        6      a    7
```

```
           R           L              R        (liftLFf)   L      R      L      R
Stamp  pu  step:  stamp  pu  step:  stamp pu  step:  (miss):    stamp:  stamp:  stamp:  stamp:
   8    a   1      a    2    a   3    a   4      (5)        a      6      a      7
```

Repeat the whole, but commencing LF

Second Eight

(The next six counts contain a similar twisting movement to the first five steps of the 'cross-over' in shim sham II)

```
 R (turn twds R)    R(turn twds L)      L          R        L        R
Stamp(w) (lightly):       heelbt:     repeat L   repeat R   stamp   stamp
        1                    2            3          4        5        6      7        8
```

```
 L     R      L     R(XfL)   L     R      L       R      L     R L
Step: shuffle: heelbt:  step:   step: step: shuffle: heelbt: step:  bll.chge
 1    a 2      a       3       4    5    a 6      a       7     a 8
```

Repeat the last sixteen counts commencing same foot but finish with two stamps (R L), feet apart.
2 3 4 5 6 7 8 1 a2 a3 a4 5 a6 a7 a8

Third Eight

```
 R     R(bsdL)  R(to R)   L    L(bsdR)  L(to L)   R     L      R     L     R      L
 pu:   ball-dig:  step:    pu:  ball-dig:  step:    pu:  heelbt:  step:  pu:  heelbt:  step:
 a      1        2        a     3        4        a    5       a     6    a       7
```
(making very small circle bkds to R)

```
   R      L (ft.apt)
Stamp:  stamp:      Repeat the whole.       Repeat once more but with one stamp at the end.
 a       8         a1 2 a3 4 a5 a6 a7 a8      a1 2 a3 4 a5 a6 a7 8
```

```
     L              R            L        R     L     R      L
Stamp  pu  step:  stamp  pu  step:  stamp  pu  step:  stamp:  stamp:  stamp:  stamp:
   1    a   2      a    3   a   4    a   5       a      6      a      7
```

Fourth Eight

```
   R      L      R(to RCF)    L       R     L     R      R L      R
Shuffle: heelbt: fwd-brush: heelbt:  step:  step:  shuffle:  bll.chge:  stamp:
   8    a   1        2         3       4     5     a 6    a 7      8
```

L   R   R L   R   L(to LCF)   R   L
Step: shuffle: bll.chge: stamp: (fwd)brush: heelbt: step: Repeat these four bars.
1   a 2 a 3   4   5   6   7

Tag
RL(fwd.ft.apart)   RL(bk.ft.tog) R(fwd)   R   L(in front)
Stamp: stamp: *(miss)* step: step: step: *(miss)* heelbt: slam
a   1   *(2)*   a   3   4   *(5)*   6   7

Leonard Reed, one of the original innovators from the beginning of the twentieth century, sharing a moment with Stephanie Smith, a young dancer of the next generation, at a tap convention. Reed's T-shirt illustrates the young Leonard Reed. (Barbara Smith)

BIBLIOGRAPHY

Alpert, Hollis, *Broadway, 125 Years of Musical Theatre* (Arcade Publishing, New York, 1999)

Atkins, Cholly, and Malone, Jacqui *Class Act, the Jazz Life of Choreographer Cholly Atkins*, 2001

Bourne, Stephen, *Black in the British Frame* (Continuum, 2001)

Carr, Roy, *A Century of Jazz* (Hamlyn, 1999)

Castle, Roy, *Roy Castle on Tap* (David & Charles, 1986)

Draper, Paul, *On Tap Dancing* (Marcel Dekker, Inc., New York and Base, 1978)

Eddleston, Pamela, *Zelia Raye and the Development of Modern Theatre Dance* (The Imperial Society of Teachers of Dancing, 2002)

Feldman, Anita, *Inside Tap* (A Dance Horizons Book, 1996)

Foley, Mark, *Dance Floors*, (Dance UK, 1998)

Forsyth, Bruce, *Bruce, the Autobiography (*Sidgwich & Jackson, 2001)

Frank, Rusty E. *Tap! The Greatest Tap Dance Stars and their Stories* (William Morrow and Company Inc., New York, 1990)

Haskins, Jim, and Mitgang, N.R., *Mr Bojangles, The Biography of Bill Robinson* (William Morrow & Company, Inc., New York, 1988)

Honri, Peter, *Working the Halls* (Saxon House, 1973)

Hudd, Roy, *Music Hall* (Eyre Methuen, London, 1976)

Jaffe, Nigel Allenby, *The World of English Folk Dance* (Folk Dance Enterprises, 1992)

Lodge, Jack, Taylor, John Russell, Turner, Adrian, Jarvis, Douglas, and Castell, David *Hollywood 50 Great Years* (PRION an imprint of Multimedia Books Ltd, 1989)

Marshall, Michael, *Top Hat and Tails, The Story of Jack Buchanan* (Elm Tree Books, London, 1978)

Mueller, John, *Astaire Dancing* (Hamish Hamilton, London)

Perry, George, *Bluebell, The Authorized Biography of Margaret Kelly, founder of the legendary Bluebell Girls* (Pavilion Books Ltd, 1997)

Snyder, Robert W., *The Voice of the City, Vaudeville and Popular Culture in New York* (Oxford University Press, 1989)

Stearns, Marshall and Jean, *Jazz Dance: The Story of American Vernacular Dance (*The Macmillan Company, New York. Collier-Macmillan Ltd, London, 1968)

Stein, Charles W., *American Vaudeville as Seen by its Contemporaries* (Da Capo Press, Inc., 1984)

The Guinness Book of Records (Guinness Publishing, London, annually)

Thomas, Bob, *Astaire the Man, The Dancer* (Weidenfeld & Nicolson, London, 1985)

Thornton, Michael, *Jessie Matthews, Biography* (Hart-Davis, MacGibbon, 1974, etc.)

Valis Hill, Constance, *Brotherhood in Rhythm: The Jazz Tap Dancing of the Nicholas Brothers* (Oxford University Press, 2000)

Vernon, Doremy, *Tiller's Girls* (Robson Books, 1988)

Useful Addresses and Magazines

Societies, Studios and Companies

British Ballet Organization, 39 Lonsdale Road, Barnes, London SW13 9JP.

British Theatre Dance Association, Leicester, LE1 3UA.

The Imperial Society of Teachers of Dancing, 22/26 Paul Street, London WC2A 4QE.

International Dance Teachers' Association, International House, 76 Bennett Road, Brighton BN2 5JL.

Council for Dance Education and Training (UK), Riverside Studios, Crisp Road, London W6 9RL.

Dance UK, 23 Crisp Road, London W4 9RL.

Dance Works, 16 Alderton Street, London W1.

Pineapple Studios, 7 Langley Street, Covent Garden, London WC2H 9JA.

Coolbeat Show Competitions and Workshops, Derek Hartley on www.stepsandnotes.com or coolbeat2k@hotmail.com

GHTap Ltd, 21 Stratford Court, Kingston Road, New Malden, London KT3 3NU.

Rees Rhythms, Master Classes, Workshops and coaching.
Heather Rees, PO Box 148, Bexhill-on-Sea, TN40 1WF.

American Tap Orchestra, 33 Little West 12th Street # 105B, New York, NY 10014.

Jazz Tap Ensemble, 1416 Westwood Blvd, Suite 207, Los Angeles, CA 90024.

Rhapsody In Taps, 4821 Matney Avenue, Long Beach, CA 90807.

International Tap Association, PO Box 356, Boulder, CO 80306.

Tap Heritage Institute (and St Louis Tap), www.tapheritage.com

Magazines

The Dancing Times, Clerkenwell House, 45–47 Clerkenwell Green, London EC1R 0EB.

Dance Express, A E Morgan Publications Ltd, Stanley House, 9 West Street, Epsom, Surrey KT18 7RL.

Dance Magazine, 111 Myrtle St. #203, Oakland, CA 94607.

Dance + Fitness, PO # 691748, W. Hollywood, CA 90069.

Dance Teacher Magazine, 250 W.57 St, Suite 420, New York, NY 10107.

CD SUPPLIERS

Second Spin, 14 Sackville Road, Bexhill-on-Sea, East Sussex, TN39 3JL.

8 & 1 Piano Company, PO Box 672, Camberley, Surrey GU16 8BB.

www.tap-dance-music.co.uk

www.hollywoodtapmall.com

DANCE WEAR SUPPLIERS
(including suppliers of costumes)

Gamba, 3 Garrick Street, Covent Garden, London WC2E 9AR.

Frederick Freed, 94 St Martin's Lane, London WC2N 4AT.

Porcelli, 9 West Street, London WC2H 9NE.

Bloch, 35 Drury Lane, Covent Garden, London WC2B 5RH.

Roch Valley, Stoneyfield Boundary Street, Rochdale OL11 3TQ.

Capezio, www.capeziodance.com

Katz, 1 Abbey Green, Nuneaton.

International Dance Supplies, 5 Shutterton Industrial Estate, Dawlish, Devon EX7 0NH.

Blochworld@www.blochworld.com

Capezio@www.capeziodance.com

Curtain Call, PO Box 709 York, PA 17405-0709. Web: www.tighe.com and email: curtaincall@ tighe.com

Art Stone, Dept DM, 1795 Express Dr North, PO Box 2505, Smithtown, NY 11787. Web: www.artstonecostume.com email: artstonedance@aol.com

FLOORS

British Harlequin plc, Bankside House, Vale Road, Tonbridge, Kent TN9 1SJ

Rosco, Roscolap Ltd, Blanchard Works, Kangley Bridge Road, Sydenham, London SE26 5AQ.

Harlequin, American Harlequin Corporation, 1531 Glen Avenue, Moorestown, NJ 08057. www.harlequinfloors.com

Rosco, Stamford, CT: 800-ROSCO NY and Hollywood, CA: 800-ROSCO LA. www.rosco.com

Woodpecker Tap Mats, AmericanTapDance-Orchestra, 33 Little West 12th St # 105B, New York, NY 10014.

Rusty Franks, www.swingshift.com/ontap.ucm

INDEX OF STEPS

GENERAL INDEX